MW01127789

Nov*
*Essential
Guide to*

CRAFTING
SCENES

Raymond Obstfeld

**WRITER'S
DIGEST
BOOKS**

Cincinnati, Ohio
www.writersdigest.com

Novelist's Essential Guide to Crafting Scenes. Copyright © 2000 by Raymond Obstfeld. Manufactured in the United States of America. All rights reserved. No part of this book may be reproduced in any form or by any electronic or mechanical means including information storage and retrieval systems without permission in writing from the publisher, except by a reviewer, who may quote brief passages in a review. Published by Writer's Digest Books, an imprint of F&W Publications, Inc., 1507 Dana Avenue, Cincinnati, Ohio, 45207. (800) 289-0963. First edition.

Visit our Web site at www.writersdigest.com for information on more resources for writers.

To receive a free weekly E-mail newsletter delivering tips and updates about writing and about Writer's Digest products, send an E-mail to newsletter-request@writersdigest.com with "Subscribe Newsletter" in the body of the message, or register directly at our Web site at www.writersdigest.com.

04   03   02   01   00   5   4   3   2   1

Library of Congress Cataloging in Publication Data

Obstfeld, Raymond.
    Novelist's essential guide to crafting scenes / by Raymond Obstfeld .
        p.   cm.
    Includes index.
    ISBN 0-89879-973-2 (pbk. : alk.paper)
    1. Fiction--Technique. 2. Creative writing. I. Title
PN3365.027 2000
808.3--dc21   00-036797

Edited by David Borcherding and Meg Leder
Cover & interior design by Matthew S. Gaynor

Excerpts from "A&P," by John Updike, are reprinted with permission of Alfred A. Knopf, a Division of Random House, Inc. Copyright © 1962 by John Updike. From *Pigeon Feathers and Other Stories.*

For British Commonwealth rights, excerpts from "A&P" by John Updike from *Pigeon Feathers and Other Short Stories* (Penguin Books, 1965), pages 130-136. Copyright © John Updike, 1959, 1960, 1961, 1962, 1965. Reproduced by permission of Penguin Books Ltd.

※

Dedication

Special thanks to the students in my novel workshop
who have made me a better teacher, writer and person.

※

ABOUT THE AUTHOR

Raymond Obstfeld is the author of twenty-seven novels in a variety of genres. He has written mysteries, suspense thrillers, mainstream and young adult novels, and these have been published in eleven languages. His novel *Dead Heat* was a finalist for an Edgar award from the Mystery Writers of America; his novel *Hungry Women* was a Literary Guild and Doubleday book club selection; and four of his novels have been optioned for movies. He has also sold ten screenplays, thirteen books of nonfiction, numerous short stories, poems and nonfiction articles. He teaches at Orange Coast College in Costa Mesa, California, and has taught at Cambridge University, the University of California—Irvine, UC—Long Beach and the University of Redlands. He lives in Tustin, California.

❈ CONTENTS ❈

WHAT A SCENE IS—
AND ISN'T

> "It doesn't matter whether you're first rate, second
> rate, or third rate, but it's of vital importance
> that the water find its own level and that you do
> the very best you can with the powers that are
> given you.... It's utterly immoral to be slothful
> about the qualities you have."
>
> Lawrence Durrell

> "The world is overstocked with people who are
> ready and eager to teach other people to write. It
> seems astonishing that so much bad writing
> should find its way into print when so much
> good advice is to be had."
>
> Robertson Davies

When asked what distinguishes a great movie, actress Rosalind
Russell simply replied, "Moments."

She meant that when we fondly think back on movies that
deeply affected us, we don't immediately recall the whole
story and all of the characters. Rather, we remember specific
highlights, moments that burned so brightly that something
inside us was illuminated and forever seared into our memory. There are countless examples of such "moments": In *On
the Waterfront*, when Marlon Brando sits on the swing and
shyly flirts with Eva Marie Saint, while nervously tugging her
tiny glove onto his massive hands; or when Brando is in the
car with Rod Steiger, explaining how he "coulda been a con-
tenda." In *Casablanca*, during the farewell at the plane when
Bogart finally lets Ingrid Bergman go. In *Lost in America*,
when Albert Brooks tries to convince the casino boss to give
back the "nest egg" his wife lost while gambling. In *There's*

Something About Mary, when Cameron Diaz borrows some of Ben Stiller's "hair gel."

These are all examples of scenes so well written that they elevate the entire work. Obviously, the more "moments" a work has, the more powerful it is. Think of each memorable scene as an inner tube designed to keep the larger work afloat. The more memorable scenes there are, the more we see the entire structure floating in front of us and, therefore, the more we appreciate the *whole* work. The fewer memorable scenes there are, the quicker that work sinks to the depths of mediocrity. And let's face it—the literary ocean floor is crowded with the debris of crappy writing.

What Is a Scene?

The word "scene" comes from theater, where it describes the action that takes place in a single physical setting. This same principle holds true in fiction: A scene might begin when characters enter a location and end when they leave, or it may take place in a single location regardless of how many characters come and go. The emotional power of a scene depends on not distracting the reader from what's going on. Too much movement between different settings can divert attention. In fact, much of a scene's power is often derived from the slightly claustrophobic feeling that the character or characters are somehow trapped in that place and must face whatever the scene is about. The setting in a scene is much like the frame around a painting: it's meant to enhance the artwork, not distract from it.

However, it is important that every writer understand that there are no firm rules to writing—only general principles. Generally, a scene takes place in one location (though the location might be moving, as with a car, train or airplane). Yet a wonderful scene could be written that spans several settings or even different dimensions. Such a scene is more complex, so its effectiveness depends on the skill of the writer.

A scene can be long or short—a paragraph or an entire chapter (see chapter six for more about length). Length doesn't define a scene—*focus* does. A scene usually focuses on a specific purpose:

- to give the reader information necessary to further plot
- to show the conflict between characters
- to develop a particular character by highlighting a specific trait or action
- to create suspense

The best scenes do a combination of the above, sometimes all of the above. What's important is that the writer (1) knows why that scene exists and (2) justifies its existence by making it memorable.

What Makes a Scene Memorable?

A scene is memorable because it catches the reader offguard. It's like playing peekaboo with an infant: As soon as he figures out the pattern of your peeking, he gets bored; to continue to amuse him, you have to vary the pattern and catch him off-guard.

Like that infant, a reader begins each scene with an expectation of what that scene will deliver—the pattern of what will happen, how it will happen and what will be said. The typical reader will have read hundreds of stories and seen thousands of hours of TV shows and movies before beginning your story. With each word his eyes consume, his mind instantly rummages through all the other stories he's ever been exposed to, looking for a match. The reader's mind is already laying out the road map of where your story is going and what the characters are going to do and say. Remember, you as the writer have also consumed thousands of stories, which are just floating around in your subconscious. They are all within easy reach when you're writing, which is why beginning writing often seems so familiar. The trick is to be aware of that inclination to steal from your storehouse of stories and to scrutinize each word to make sure it's your own. While it is inevitable that your story will have similarities to many others, it shouldn't duplicate them. Your job is to make

> # TIP
> ### The "So-What" Factor
> *When you finish reading a scene, ask yourself, "So what? Is this scene necessary?" Read the scenes before and after the one in question and ask yourself if it really matters. Does whatever happens deserve its own scene? Could the information be placed in one of the neighboring scenes?*

each scene an unexpected experience for the reader. Either the dialogue is fresh, the situation is unusual or the style is so wonderful that it elevates even the most predictable scene to a new height of intensity.

In fact, you can use the reader's knowledge of plots to your advantage because you can know what his expectations are. In *Psycho*, director Alfred Hitchcock purposely cast a famous star (Janet Leigh) in the role of the doomed shower-taker. He knew that the audience wouldn't expect anything bad to happen to her so early in the film. Since then, so many filmmakers have copied that ploy that it's lost its effectiveness. In the film *Marathon Man* (based on William Goldman's suspense novel), Babe (Dustin Hoffman) is held captive by evil Nazis who are torturing him. He's just an average guy, a grad student, up against ruthless professionals, so the audience knows he has no chance to escape on his own. His only hope is the professional spy Janeway (William Devane). And, in fact, Janeway does rescue Babe, killing his captors and speeding off in the getaway car. While speeding away, Janeway explains to Babe why he's been kidnapped and questions him about any knowledge he has about the bad guys. When Babe, hiding on the floor in the back, cries out that he knows nothing, the car screeches to a halt and Babe discovers he's right back with his tormentors, who only faked being dead. Janeway is in on it with them. It's a neat scene because it plays on the audience's expectations of escape, while at the same time snatching it away. Babe is now on his own and the audience doesn't know how he'll get out of it. An additional bonus of the scene is that the author explains the complex plot to the audience so they know what's been going on. (In fact, the scene is so good that the more recent movie, *Enemy of the State*, copies it, this time with Gabriel Byrne as the phony rescuer and Will Smith as the trusting dupe.)

A Leap of Faith

While it's crucial that the completed scene accomplishes one of the focuses listed above, it's not crucial that you know any of that when you start the scene. Sometimes when you have a sudden idea for a scene in an offbeat setting, it's best to just start writing. Don't overthink or overplan it. Jump in with fingers flying. Don't worry that you aren't sure what will happen or why the characters are there. It's enough that you think it would make a good scene in the book.

In other words, just write it.

Some of the best scenes are memorable because they were spontaneous ideas. The author wonders, "What would happen if I stuck my characters in the teacup ride at Disneyland? That would be cool." And she starts writing the scene. Later, when that initial burst of inspiration wears off (and believe me, it does), the author will have to start asking questions about the scene: Why is it here? What do I hope to accomplish with it? How can I best utilize this odd setting? The author may decide this would be the perfect setting for the scene in which the couple discusses getting a divorce. At first the author was going to set the divorce-discussion scene in the couple's kitchen while they prepared dinner, but now they are sitting in a spinning teacup talking about their divorce while their children ride in the teacup next to them. The contrast of their children laughing in the "happiest place on earth" while the parents discuss visitation adds impact to the scene. The sensation of spinning while they dismantle the stability of their lives and the lives of their children can make the reader experience the physical emotions that the characters might be going through. Plus, you have the thematic irony of the children being thrilled at the controlled chaos of spinning just as they are about to experience the wrenching pain of the uncontrolled real thing.

But the writer didn't know all that when she started the scene—she just thought it was a neat idea. A weak writer will be satisfied with that. A good writer will then transform the "neat idea" into a fully realized scene, rich with nuance, texture, character and theme.

Look Out Behind You!

Just as with a good magician, the key to the writer's art is *misdirection*. Though every scene has a purpose or focus, the best scenes achieve this subtlety through misdirection. You want the reader to be looking at one hand while you distract her with the other. This is especially important if the scene exists merely to deliver information. As we saw with the scene from *Marathon Man*, Goldman (who also wrote the screenplay) misdirects the audience to focus on the suspense of the getaway while casually delivering crucial information that the audience doesn't notice it's getting. Imagine how boring the scene would be if it were just two people sitting at a table with one of them explaining what's going on.

Another example of misdirection comes in the opening scene of Elmore Leonard's *LaBrava*. Two characters are discussing the photography of the protagonist, Joe LaBrava, who has not yet appeared in the novel. (This technique of introducing a main character through others is discussed in "The Buddy System" section of chapter two.) While his agent discusses how great the photos are, the readers come to understand LaBrava's character. But this brief five-page chapter wants to do more. Now that it has the reader wondering if the agent, Maurice, will convince the gallery owner, Evelyn, to offer a showing of LaBrava's photographs, Leonard is able to unload character description and background. (*Note*: The first speaker is Maurice, LaBrava's agent.)

> *"This guy's for real, and he's gonna make it. I guarantee you."*
> *"Is he presentable?"*
> *"Nice looking guy, late thirties. Dark hair, medium height, on the thin side. No style, but yeah, he's presentable."*
>
> *Evelyn said, "I see 'em come in with no socks on, I know they've got a portfolio full of social commentary."*
>
> *"He's not a hippy. No, I didn't mean to infer that." Maurice paused, serious, about to confide. "You know the guys that guard the President? The Secret Service guys? That's what he used to be, one of those."*

See what happened while you were busy looking at the photographs? She asks if he's presentable so she can sell his work, and Leonard has an excuse to describe him. She questions Maurice's description, and Leonard has an excuse to tell you about his Secret Service background.

The teacup scene described earlier does the same thing. While the reader is focused on the sensual experience of the

amusement park—the spinning cups, the laughing children—
the actual point of the scene, the divorce discussion, is more
interesting and involving. This is not to say a simple scene of
two people sitting at a table can't be compelling—it most certainly can—but once again, its effectiveness still depends on
some other element being exceptional: prose style, dialogue or
characterization.

Final Word
Any work of art is made up of smaller parts, just as a novel,
story or script is made up of scenes. What's interesting about
any completed work of art is that the final product is greater
than the sum of its smaller parts. In this way, the work is like
a family, community or country. A scene is like a single member of a family: It is loved for its own individuality, but its great-
est power is its contribution to the larger group.

Therefore, when beginning to write a scene, you must concentrate only on the elements that make that scene work as an
isolated ministry. Later, when you have the story completed,
you must judge each scene's effectiveness according to how
much it contributes to the whole work.

Instant Workshop:
Focus

Still can't decide whether or not the scene you've just written belongs in your story? Here's help: Read the scene again and when
you're finished, complete the following sentences:

1. The Plot Focus
The purpose of this scene is to

_____

_____

Example: The purpose of this scene is to reveal the protagonist's
childhood abuses in order to provide motivation for her current
actions.

2. The Character Focus
When the reader finishes this scene, he should feel

_____

_____

_____

Example: When the reader finishes this scene, he should feel sympathy for the protagonist, yet be skeptical of her reliability as a narrator.

3. The Theme Focus
When the reader finishes this scene, he should think

_____

_____

_____

Example: When the reader finishes this scene, he should think that the protagonist has been using these abuses as an excuse for many other self-destructive actions.

4. The Suspense Focus
When the reader finishes this scene, he should wonder

_____

_____

_____

Example: When the reader finishes this scene, he should wonder whether or not the protagonist will be able to overcome the horror of her childhood in order to reunite with her estranged mother.

❀ 2 ❀

JUMP RIGHT IN—
THE WORDS ARE FINE:
STARTING A SCENE

> *"One of the most difficult things is the first para-*
> *graph. I have spent many months on a first*
> *paragraph and once I get it, the rest comes out*
> *very easily. In the first paragraph you solve most*
> *of the problems of your book. The theme is de-*
> *fined, the style, the tone."*
>
> Gabriel García Márquez

> *"I always start a novel by writing its first page and*
> *its last page, which seem to survive almost intact*
> *through all the following drafts and changes."*
>
> Jerzy Kosinski, author of *Being There*

A scene is just like a complete story or novel in that it has a beginning, middle and ending. Each of these three components
has its own job to do in order to insure the scene's success.
Even though the completed story or novel may include dozens
or even hundreds of scenes, the structure of each individual
scene remains the same: beginning, middle, ending.

Think of a scene as if it were an average day in your work-
week. Even though you may have different duties during the
day, the structure of your day is generally the same.

Beginning: prepare for the day by washing, dressing and
eating
Middle: go to your job or school
Ending: come home, eat, spend time with the family, relax,
watch TV

Certainly there are variations in that plan, but it's basically the same division of time for most people. Although the structure of each day is similar, the days themselves aren't. Neither are individual scenes. Some days, like some scenes, are more interesting, exciting and fulfilling than others. Sometimes, if the day begins just right, the rest of the day can be better. It is the same with a scene.

The beginning of a scene has only one mission: hook the reader. It must make that reader want to keep reading. Of course, it could introduce conflict, establish stakes or develop theme, but those could come anywhere in a scene. When we send that wide-eyed young Beginning out into the battlefield of the literary world, we ask it to do one job for author and country: bring back the reader alive—and wanting more.

One way to look at the beginning of a scene is to treat it as if it were a blind date. The reader is the date sitting at the table waiting for you. He or she is gorgeous—your dream date—and you want to make a good impression as soon as you meet. You know the first words out of your mouth will set the tone for the rest of the evening. So what do you say?

"At Least Nothing Was Broken"

You could start with, "I was born in a small town in Pennsylvania, in a red brick hospital on a snowy January...." Of course, by the time you finish this sentence, there's a good chance you'll be sitting by yourself. Unless you're a witness being interrogated by a cop, it's not always a good idea to begin at the beginning. Sometimes it's better to begin in the middle. Naturally, there's a Latin term for it so we college teachers can sound smarter: *in media res* (beginning in the middle). All that means is first grab my interest and make me care before you give me all the intricate details.

Here's an example of *in media res*. John Updike's classic short story "A&P" begins like this:

> *In walk these three girls in nothing but bathing suits. I'm in the third checkout slot, with my back to the door, so I don't see them until they're over by the bread. The one that caught my eye first was the one in the plaid green two-piece.*

Updike begins his story with the *plot conflict*, the catalyst that ignites the story's action. Had he begun at the "beginning," his story might have started like this:

> *One summer many years ago, when I was only nineteen, I worked in the local A&P grocery store as a checkout boy. Each day I would arise, put on the white shirt my mother had ironed for me the night before, grab the lunch bag she'd prepared for me that morning, and walk the five blocks along the shore to work.*

There's nothing technically wrong with this version. It introduces a character and his situation, while telling us he's still somewhat dependent on his mother (the information about his mother ironing his shirts comes out later in Updike's story). However, it's a passive opening, lazily unraveling like someone telling you a dream.

Updike's opening is much more dynamic and complex. The first line—"In walk these three girls in nothing but bathing suits"—startles us because we don't yet know the setting. This creates a minisuspense hook. Second, the narrator's tone is obviously one of shock, so the reader's suspense is heightened. Third, the suddenness of the action and the narrator's response reflects his manic state of mind—he's a jumpy kid unhappy with his job and life, but unsure why. Fourth, the grammar of the first sentence (and subsequent sentences) is not technically correct, so we subtly learn something about the narrator's education. This last item is crucial to the theme because Sammy, the narrator, comes to a self-realization later on that is the result of an active moral choice, not merely thinking about the situation. He does what's right because it "feels" right, not because he intellectually analyzed the conflict. In one short sentence, Updike manages to accomplish all of these things.

Updike's story begins with the action that causes the reaction. Another place to begin could be immediately *after* the action that sets the story in motion. In William Goldman's *Heat*, he begins with:

> *At least nothing was broken.*
> *She knew that. No. The savaging had been so sudden, the*

> *imparting of pain so skilled, that she knew precious little.*
> *But nothing was broken; she sensed that.*

In this case, starting with her beating might have repelled the reader. It's more important that she cares about the person than knows the details of the beating. The reader has to like her because everything that happens in the novel is based on the fact that the hero likes her. So although Goldman began *in media res*, he didn't need to show the violence.

Either of the above openings—the active *in media res* or the passive once-upon-a-time—could work. Which one you choose depends upon what tone, pace, characterization and so on that you wish to establish.

Say What?

Beginning a scene with a dialogue exchange is a variation on the above *in media res*. This, too, begins in the middle of the action, only the action is conversation. The advantage is that the reader is stepping into something ongoing, so there is already an established momentum to sweep the reader along. There is also the suspense of figuring out the context of the conversation, the same as if you were eavesdropping on the table next to yours in a restaurant. In addition, conversation is an interesting and subtle way to present characterization very quickly. For example, the first scene in my novel *Earth Angel* begins with dialogue:

> "I read somewhere," Carol said, kneeling to wipe blood from the
> floor, "that a couple years ago they had an auction in Paris
> where a guy bought Napoleon's penis."
>> I laughed. "Napoleon's schlong?"
>> "I'm not kidding. They auctioned it off. All these guys in
> expensive suits and silk ties tugging their ears or scratching
> their noses to bid for a severed dick. Does that seem weird or
> what?"

Originally, I'd started the novel with a different conversation, but when I read about this auction in the newspaper, I knew it was a natural conversation topic for these two women. Here's what I wanted to accomplish:

1. Show that they were good friends, able to talk in a joking manner about anything
2. Show that they were mature women not embarrassed by the racy subject matter
3. Establish a humorous tone, which is important because something very serious is about to happen (the humorous tone will help create a greater sense of shock and disorientation in the reader when the event happens because she'll be caught offguard)
4. Have them talk about an actual event that the reader would find interesting
5. Have a conversation so bizarre that the reader will want to know where it could possibly lead
6. Introduce a suspense element (wiping blood from the floor), but increasing the suspense by not yet telling the reader how the blood got there

Here are a couple examples of dialogue openings from Leonard Michaels's stories:

> *I said, "Ikstein stands outside the door for a long time before he knocks. Did you suspect that? Did you suspect that he stands there listening to what we say before he knocks?" She said, "Did you know you're crazy?"*
> from "Something Evil"

> *"Philip," she said, "this is crazy."*
> *I didn't agree or disagree. She wanted some answer. I bit her neck.*
> from "City Boy"

In both examples, kicking the scene off with dialogue creates immediate momentum and interest because the reader wants to know more about the situation that prompts the dialogue. This is an especially attractive technique to many writers because they are able to deliver characterization, background information, plot conflict and more, all while the reader is distracted by the flow of conversation. For just this reason, author Gregory McDonald begins most of his scenes with dialogue in all of his *Fletch* novels.

The Jump Cut

Although the above examples involve opening scenes, this same *in media res* technique can be used in scenes throughout a story or novel. Some writers begin every chapter this way in order to keep a sense of urgency to the plot. The first line is some action or dialogue that has nothing to do with the previous scene even though the same characters are involved. This creates a sense of suspense—the reader must now find out what happened between the time the last scene ended and this one began. Here's another example from *Earth Angel*. The last sentence of chapter seven is, "I cried all the way over the Rockies until a flight attendant knocked and asked if I needed help." Chapter eight begins:

> *"This can't possibly work," he argued, twisting his napkin's neck for emphasis. "You'll just end up embarrassing me."*
> *"You have to trust me," I said.*
> *"I do?" He frowned.*

There is no apparent relationship between the ending of chapter seven and the opening of chapter eight. The suspense is what happened after her flight landed. Who is this man she's talking to? What "can't possibly work"? Will she get him to trust her? Is trusting her a mistake? In movies, this is called a jump cut, although fiction writers employed it long before there were movies. However, the influence of movies on fiction writing can't be ignored and this technique has become more popular.

Here's another example from Jen Banbury's novel, *Like a Hole in the Head*. The last lines of one chapter focus on a fight in which a man attacks the female narrator:

> *...I kicked out again, this time connecting with his lame wrist. He screamed and rolled over into a fetal position. I pushed myself up so I was squatting on the chair, facing him. I flipped the catch on the gun and yelled, "The safety's off! The safety is off! Do you hear me? You jerk you fucking jerk? It's fucking off!" I let out a single sob, then held it all in.*

The chapter ends there. The reader is left wondering what will happen next: Will she pull the trigger? Will she force him to reveal the whereabouts of the object she's after? The intensity is especially high at the end of this chapter because she's yelling and sobbing, showing that she's at an emotional edge. Also, the reader knows her life is at stake and she's not good with guns—a volatile combination. But the next chapter doesn't answer the reader's questions. Instead, it starts with, "I was making good time until I ran out of gas a couple of miles outside Baker." Now there is a separate conflict (running out of gas) to add to wondering what happened to the guy she was pointing a gun at. The author used the jump cut to double the suspense.

The "Big Promise" Opening

Another technique for beginning a scene is to make a promise about what the following scene will do. The greater the impact of the claim, the greater the reader's interest in the scene. Here are a few examples of possible "big claim" openings:

1. *When I awoke that morning, I had no idea that this was the beginning of the day that would destroy my family, ruin my career and put my face on every newspaper in the country.*

2. *What Sasha did next changed everything I'd ever believed about romantic love.*

3. *Johnny burst into my office, tossed the briefcase on my desk and laughed hysterically. "Go ahead. Open it. But before you do, walk into your boss's office and quit this stupid job. Because once you open that case, man, nothing will ever be the same."*

Those are fairly melodramatic examples, but the technique is the same even when it is more modest. Technically, Updike's "A&P" discussed earlier is one continuous scene in which the three girls walk around the grocery store, get yelled at by the conservative store manager and leave just as Sammy quits in protest. But Updike deliberately puts a break in the story. He divides the story into two parts, two separate scenes, even though we are still in the same setting and basic sequence of action.

So why divide this into two scenes? Since you can't answer the question without reading the entire story, I'll help you out.

The two scenes aren't divided according to action as much as they are divided according to Sammy's change in character. In the first scene, Sammy is a superficial teenage boy who is dissatisfied with his job, although he can't articulate why. The first scene is filled with Sammy's shallow observations: Referring to girls' minds, he quips, "Do you really think it's a mind in there or just a little buzz like a bee in a glass jar?" One of the reasons Sammy can't escape his crappy job at the A&P (and is doomed to live the same lives as the customers he hates) is because he only sees the physical and judges people solely on appearances. But when he sees how the A&P staff mistreats the girls, he recognizes himself in the staff's behavior and decides to change.

The last line before the break is, "Poor kids, I began to feel sorry for them, they couldn't help it." The line immediately after the break is, "Now here comes the sad part of the story, at least my family says it's sad, but I don't think it's so sad myself." The last line before the break shows that Sammy has switched allegiances from the judgmental crowd that runs the A&P to the kind of person who has his own views of what's right and wrong. The line after the break, which begins the final scene, further demonstrates that because he doesn't agree with the A&P, what happens next is sad.

What's interesting here is that Updike didn't need a break in the story (in fact, in some versions, the break has been removed); the story would have progressed nicely on the momentum of the action. Therefore, he broke it into two scenes for a reason. The first reason is thematic to emphasize the change in Sammy. The second reason is technique to increase the suspense. Starting the second scene with "Now here comes the sad part of the story"

TIP

How to Mark Scene Breaks

When typing your story, always indicate a break by typing a marker. For example, when you finish the last sentence before the break, hit the return twice, type three asterisks (* * *), center them, then hit the return twice to begin the next section. You need to type something that clearly marks the break because simply skipping lines can be confusing. If the extra lines appear at the beginning or end of a manuscript page, the editor might not notice the break. Also, when you first create a break, it may not be at the beginning or end of a page, but once you start editing, adding or cutting, the break will move around.

creates suspense as to what will happen next. The reader has already been warned that whatever happens next will be dramatic, a life-changing event, and Sammy's comment on the future perks up her attention as she continues. It's like a caffeine boost in the middle of the day when you're starting to sag.

If You Really Must Begin at the Beginning

Having made a case for beginning in the middle, let's look at the advantages of beginning at the beginning. I didn't start with this option because so many beginning writers use it poorly. They start at the beginning sometimes due to laziness (they don't want to take the time or effort to create a more compelling opening) and sometimes due to ignorance (they don't know what their options are). I can help with the second problem.

First, you need to clarify where the "beginning" is. Is it the birth of a character? The birth of one of the protagonist's ancestors? Or, as in some of James Michener's novels, is the beginning when the earth was still molten? The answer is the same to most questions about writing: It depends on what you're trying to achieve. The following are some options.

SETTING

You might begin with a description of the setting—or the primordial formation of the land—if the setting itself is a crucial "character" in the story or scene. (For more on the use of setting, see chapter four.) By starting with the description of a place, you are announcing to the reader that the setting is not just backdrop, but an active influence on the characters and action in this scene. The following paragraph opens chapter twelve of David Guterson's novel, *Snow Falling on Cedars*:

> Outside the wind blew steadily from the north, driving snow against the courthouse. By noon three inches had settled on the town, a snow so ethereal it could hardly be said to have settled at all; instead it swirled like some icy fog, like the breath of ghosts, up and down Amity Harbor's streets—powdery dust devils, frosted puffs of ivory cloud, spiraling tendrils of white smoke. By noon the smell of the sea was eviscerated, the sight of it mistily deplet-

> ed, too; one's field of vision narrowed in close, went blurry and snowbound, fuzzy and opaque, the sharp scent of frost burned in the nostrils of those who ventured out of doors. The snow flew up from their boots as they struggled, heads down, toward Peterson's Grocery. When they looked out into the whiteness of the world the wind flung it sharply at their narrowed eyes and foreshortened their view of everything.

Why this rich and lengthy description of snow? Because Guterson wants the reader to understand that the snow isn't just frozen water; it's a cosmic force that puts the people in the community he's writing about—as well as the murder trial that the novel is about—in perspective. The snow, which is described as "ghosts" and "devils," suggests an indifferent universe that doesn't care about human notions of right and wrong. Therefore, the only justice in the world is that which the people provide. The key phrase here is, "...the whiteness of the world the wind flung it sharply at their narrowed eyes and foreshortened their view of everything." It describes the effect of the natural world on the people involved in the trial: It blinds them. In this way, setting not only establishes the weather, but also underscores the theme of the book.

TIME

Another popular place to begin is based on the time of day rather than location. Many novice (and some experienced) writers like to start where their own lives begin each day—when they wake up. It's a natural place to start: A character awakens from a sleep that ends the old daily routine and begins an adventure that changes his life. The danger of this "I woke up to the screaming alarm clock" opening is that it's cliché. However, in the hands of a good writer, even a cliché can be revitalized. Here are two examples:

> I woke up with a hangover and roof tar on my feet and a vague recollection of pacing around up there half the night. I think I threw a bottle at the building next door and somebody yelled something.
>
> from *Like a Hole in the Head*
> by Jen Banbury

Women on their own run in Alice's family. This dawns on her with the unkindness of a heart attack and she sits up in bed to get a closer look at her thoughts, which have collected above her in the dark.

from *Pigs in Heaven*
by Barbara Kingsolver

While both are good openings that begin with waking up in bed, they each work in a different way. Banbury's opening is *suggestive*. She merely lists details: hangover, roof tar on feet, vague memory, throwing a bottle, someone yelling. These details create suspense. The reader wants to know two things: What happened last night, and why did the narrator do those things?

Kingsolver's opening is more *internal*, with a more elaborate style. Rather than giving out details, it starts with a pronouncement: "Women on their own run in Alice's family." The reader is immediately alerted to theme: the nature of women on their own. The author emphasizes this through the use of simile ("This dawns on her with the unkindness of a heart attack") and imagery ("her thoughts, which have collected above her in the dark"). Employing simile and imagery in the opening tells us that a richer style will be emphasized, sometimes the sign of a more "literary" work.

Both openings are equally suspenseful, but in different ways. The immediate suspense level is not as high in Kingsolver's opening because there's no promise of finding out what happened. Instead, the focus is on the long run: why these women are on their own and how it affects them.

This technique of beginning with the protagonist waking up is usually used in the opening scene or chapter of a story, but it can be used anywhere. When used as an opening scene, it immediately plunges the reader into a character's life and world. If he wakes up in his own room, the reader gets to see how he lives. If he wakes up somewhere else, the reader understands a different aspect of his life. If the technique is used in a scene later in the story, it can indicate a contrast in the character's life. Perhaps she was a happy person who's just suffered an emotional setback. Seeing how she wakes up and goes about her day can reveal how she has been affected by all that has happened in the story. The best part of this technique is that you show rather than tell us how she feels.

ACTION

The other place to begin is to introduce us to the action that causes the rest of the story—the Prime Mover, so to speak. For example, you might open with a car crash. Perhaps the story is not about the people in the crash, but how the crash affected all of the people who saw it, as in Karl Shapiro's poem, "Auto Wreck." (Yes, poems also have scenes.) The action can be dramatic, as in the car crash, or seemingly innocent, as in Richard Wilbur's "A Game of Catch":

> *Monk and Glennie were playing catch on the side lawn of the firehouse when Scho caught sight of them. They were good at it, for seventh-graders, as anyone could see right away. Monk, wearing a catcher's mitt, would lean easily sidewise and back, with one leg lifted and his throwing hand almost down to the grass, and then lob the white ball straight up into the sunlight.*

Looks innocent enough—a couple of kids playing catch. That's what Wilbur wants you to see: two boys in a sort of paradise. But as the story progresses, he slowly reveals a darker side to their game and its affect on all three boys. By the end, their lives have been changed all because of this simple game of catch presented in the opening scene.

This opening from Stephen Dixon's "The Signing" is a more direct example of beginning with the catalyst action:

> *My wife dies. Now I'm alone. I kiss her hands and leave the hospital room. A nurse runs after me as I walk down the hall.*
> > *"Are you going to make arrangements now for the deceased?" he says.*
> > *"No."*

The death of the narrator's wife prompts the activity that follows, which is not about her death, but how the narrator grieves. The author focuses our attention on this through the staccato style. The quick, choppy sentences indicate his disorientation. The nurse turning out to be male, while not uncommon, still momentarily surprises the reader. Just as the reader is again surprised a few lines later when the doctor speaking to him is identified as a woman. Dixon is using the reader's preconceptions to jolt her, to disorient her so she can experience just a little of what the narrator is experiencing.

How is opening with an action different than opening *in media res?* The latter refers to beginning in the middle of a plot already in motion. The former refers to beginning with an action that *causes* the plot. It's a subtle distinction and not one to get too wrapped up in. More important than labels is starting your story in such a way that it makes the reader want to keep reading.

The Buddy System

I've got this friend who can tell you precisely what's in your wallet within two minutes of meeting you. Right down to the exact amount of money and which credit cards you have. Even who's in your photos.

Don't believe me? Want to meet her?

Of course you don't believe me, but of course you want to meet her.

That's how the "buddy system" technique works. You begin a scene with someone describing another character—usually the main character. The person describing this character can be the first-person narrator of the story or just a secondary character. One advantage of this technique is that it builds immediate suspense about the character being discussed. The opening chapter of Elmore Leonard's *LaBrava* doesn't include the main character, Joe LaBrava (as discussed in the "Look Out Behind You!" section of chapter one). It's a five-page scene in which LaBrava's elderly agent Maurice tries to sell his client's photographs to art dealer Evelyn. It's through his detailed description of the photos that the reader comes to understand LaBrava's character:

> "He's been taking pictures three years, look at the work," Maurice said. "Here, this guy. Look at the pose, the expression. Who's he remind you of?"

> *"He looks like a hustler," the woman said.*
>
> *"He is a hustler, the guy's a pimp. But that's not what I'm talking about. Here, this one. Exotic dancer backstage. Remind you of anyone?"*
>
> *"The girl?"*
>
> *"Come on, Evelyn, the shot. The feeling he gets. The girl trying to look lovely, showing you her treasures, and they're not bad. But look at the dressing room, all the glitzy crap, the tinfoil cheapness."*

Maurice is showing her (and the reader) that LaBrava is an artist, has an eye for contrasts and irony, sees more about people than the average person. As the discussion continues, the reader also finds out what he looks like and that he was once with the Secret Service. All this detail boosts the reader's desire to meet him.

In Stanley Elkin's "A Poetics for Bullies," Eugene, the sidekick to the protagonist, Push the Bully, arrives at Push's house to excitedly describe a new kid in the neighborhood—the story's antagonist. This begins the second scene of the story, with the first scene being Push's three-page self-description of what it takes to be a bully (see "Character Description" later).

> *One day Eugene Kraftsman rang my bell. Eugene is afraid of me so he helps me. He's fifteen and there's something wrong with his saliva glands and he drools. His chin is always chapped. I tell him he has to drink a lot because he loses so much water. "Push? Push," he says. He's wiping his chin with his tissues.*
>
> *"Push, there's this kid—"*
>
> *"Better get a glass of water, Eugene."*
>
> *"No, Push, no fooling, there's this new kid—he just moved in. You've got to see this kid."*
>
> *"Eugene, get some water, please. You're drying up...."*
>
> *"All right, Push, but then you've got to see—"*
>
> *"Swallow, Eugene. You better swallow."*
>
> *He gulps hard.*
>
> *"Push, this is a kid and a half. Wait, you'll see."*

Don't you want to see this new kid now? What's interesting here is that Elkin not only makes you want to meet this character, he uses the same withholding technique to develop Push's character. The suspense is enhanced by Push not letting Eugene talk about the kid, in turn delaying the information to the reader. This makes the reader anxious to hear more. At the same time, Push's interruptions reveal his character—a boy who is more interested in dominating Eugene than listening to him. The best writers take advantage of such techniques to do more than one thing at a time.

A variation of this technique involves the first-person story told from the point of view of someone other than the main character. Seems like a contradiction, doesn't it? If someone's telling the story, isn't he or she the protagonist? True, unless the story's focus is another character, often mentioned in the title as with *The Great Gatsby* or *What Makes Sammy Run?* Such stories focus on this main character as an enigma who must be unraveled. Each scene, therefore, is designed to further reveal another angle of the main character, but from the narrator's limited perspective. It's like a jigsaw puzzle in which each scene is a piece of the puzzle with the narrator and reader both discovering the final picture together. The opening scene of *What Makes Sammy Run?* reveals our first glimpse at Sammy through the narrator's eyes:

> *The first time I saw him he couldn't have been much more than sixteen years old, a little ferret of a kid, sharp and quick. Sammy Glick. Used to run copy for me. Always ran. Always looked thirsty.*

Why is Sammy like this? What will become of such a boy? How will it affect the narrator? Those are the implied questions in the opening; the suspense of the novel is the slow revelation of the answers. (Note also how the clipped style emulates Sammy's on-the-go personality, as if Sammy has already begun to influence the narrator.)

Because this technique is basically like a mystery story, it is widely used in the mystery genre. It allows the writer to withhold information from the reader. This is especially popular in mystery stories featuring a brilliant detective. Having the side-kick tell the story (as Watson does in the Sherlock Holmes mysteries and Archie Goodwin does in the Nero Wolfe mysteries) heightens the suspense since the reader isn't allowed inside the detective's head. Whenever the detective tells the narrator to do something unusual, the narrator wonders—for the reader—why in blazes he wants me to do this.

Character Description: "I'm the Kinda Guy Who..."

A popular way of opening a scene is with character description—not so much describing the character's physical attributes, but more her personality, particularly focusing on some aspect of her personality that will influence the plot and theme of the story. There are two main categories of character description: (1) self-description through first-person point of view, or (2) description through third-person point of view.

SELF-DESCRIPTION

The advantage of the first-person method is that it allows you the additional opportunity to show an unreliable narrator (see chapter four for more on use of point of view). The character can describe herself, but because of how she describes herself, the reader knows not to trust her perspective. You've probably run into someone who says, "I'm the kind of person who..." and then goes on to tell you some trait of his. How often have you realized, even as he describes himself, that he isn't that kind of person at all, as the story he's telling clearly illustrates? This is true of Holden Caulfield in *The Catcher in the Rye*; the more he tells, the more the reader realizes that he doesn't really understand what's happening to him. Even though the same unreliable narrator can be created in the third-person point of view, the effect is less personal and the reader is more removed from the experience. For example, in the opening to Updike's "A&P" presented earlier, the reader quickly realizes that Sammy tells the truth as far as he knows it, but because he's so immature, it's not the same truth that the reader sees. Sammy describes people and things only in terms of their appearance, which the reader quickly realizes is how he views the world—and incorrectly so. The story describes how he finally sees beyond the surface to discover himself. The suspense for the reader is, "Will Sammy reach that level of self-discovery that will free him?" This is basically the same question we ask of Richard Dreyfuss's character in the film *American Graffiti* and Matthew Modine's character in *Vision Quest*. But this suspense only exists if the reader recognizes that the narrator has a skewed perspective and doesn't realize which is the best choice.

However, not all narrators are unreliable. They describe themselves accurately even if the reader doesn't like what she sees. Stanley Elkin's "A Poetics for Bullies" begins with Push describing himself:

> *I'm Push the bully, and what I hate are new kids and sissies, dumb kids and smart, rich kids, poor kids, kids who wear glasses, talk funny, show off, patrol boys and wise guys and kids who pass pencils and water the plants—and cripples, especially cripples. Nobody loved I love.*

Clearly this is not a politically correct opening, but if you only look at the list, you miss the point, which is the last line: *Nobody loved I love.* Even though he describes himself as a bully, that last line tells us that he's not motivated by hate but by love. Though that seems contradictory, the brilliance of the story is how the reader is reluctantly dragged along behind this dynamic character only to be won over by him after she recognizes his full nature. By the end of the story, he is in fact heroic even though he is still a bully.

Martin Amis begins his novel, *The Rachel Papers*, by having the narrator give a lengthy physical description of himself:

> *My name is Charles Highway, though you wouldn't think it to look at me. It's such a rangy, well-travelled, big-cocked name and, to look at me, I am none of these. I wear glasses for a start, have done since I was nine. And my medium-length, arseless waistless figure, corrugated rib cage and bandy legs gang up to dispel any hint of aplomb.*

The paragraph continues for more than half the page, revealing his self-deprecating attitude about his physical shortcomings. In this way, the reader not only learns what the narrator looks like, but that he's unhappy with his looks. And, in fact, since his self-loathing is the heart of what the novel is about, the reader is introduced to the theme.

THIRD-PERSON POINT OF VIEW DESCRIPTION

The advantage of using the third-person point of view for a character description is that, because it is more remote, the author's subtle judgment of the character comes through.

> *When she was young, Mary saw a brilliant and original man lose his job because he had expressed ideas that were offensive to the trustees of the college where they both taught. She shared his views, but did not sign the protest petition. She was, after all, on trial herself—as a teacher, as a woman, as an interpreter of history.*
> from *In the Garden of the North American Martyrs*
> by Tobias Wolff

Now, reread this paragraph, replacing the name Mary and each pronoun relating to Mary with I, me or my. Were this in first-person point of view, the reader might be inclined to accept the narrator's version, but because the third-person allows the narrator's tone to come through, the reader sees right away that Mary is kidding herself. The fact that Mary realizes she is "on trial" by the school but doesn't realize she's also "on trial" in the bigger arena of moral behavior points out the irony that she is a lousy "interpreter of history," since she overlooks the very lesson about moral choice that history teaches us. Therefore, Mary's life echoes Santayana's famous observation, "Those who cannot remember the past are condemned to repeat it." As the rest of the story unfolds, that's exactly what Mary comes to understand.

Danger, Will Robinson: Dream Sequence Ahead!

Imagine yourself at home on a Sunday afternoon watching TV and snacking when suddenly the doorbell rings. You answer it, and it's Ed McMahon with a check for eight million dollars made out in your name! There are TV cameras, confetti and a brass band, and you're thinking, "Finally, no more month-to-month living. I can buy a car that actually runs, I can tell my boss who's been harassing me to shove it and my mother can finally have that lifesaving heart surgery she needs." Then Ed McMahon rips off his face and it's Peter Funt from *Candid Camera*. Everybody's laughing at the great joke they just pulled on you. The cameras are packed away, the confetti swept up and you return to your snack of Spam and saltines.

If you can imagine your disappointment at that moment, then you can imagine how a reader feels after she's read an exciting cliff-hanging opening in which a character is in some death-defying situation with no apparent way out. Breathlessly, the reader turns the page only to find the inevitable words, "...and then Cameron woke up. It was just a dream." Then the character gets up and the real story begins.

You, too, would be disappointed and probably angered by such a cheap trick. So are your readers. Unless the dream is integral to your story, don't open with it.

Having made the warning, I will also admit that there have been stories I've read that opened with a dream sequence that actually worked. Here is the opening scene in Donald Barthelme's *Paradise*:

> *After the women had gone Simon began dreaming with new intensity. He dreamed that he was a slave on a leper island, required to clean latrines and pile up dirty-white shell for the roads, wheelbarrow after wheelbarrow, then rake the shell smooth and jump up and down on it until it was packed solid. The lepers did not allow him to wear shoes, only white athletic socks, and he had a difficult time finding a pair that matched. The head leper, a man who seemed to be named Al, embraced him repeatedly and tried repeatedly to spit in his mouth.*

One obvious difference with Barthelme's opening is that he tells the reader right up front that this is a dream, so there's no letdown. Second, the tone is comical, so that even if the reader hadn't been told, she'd know that this was not a situation to take seriously.

The main reason writers play the "it was a dream" card is because they can't think of a legitimately interesting way to open the scene without this gimmick. Sometimes it is used to open a scene or chapter later in a novel to show the stress that the character has been feeling. Fine. But by setting it up as if it were real action, you risk yanking the reader out of the novel because she is so disappointed at the contrived device.

Final Word

As you can see, there are a variety of options in starting a scene. How do you know which is the best for your particular scene?

You don't.

Sometimes you begin a scene a certain way and it's perfect, just what you'd hoped for. But other times you have to try several different approaches. This is especially true if you have a tendency to begin all or most of your scenes the same way, which can set up a monotonous rhythm in your story. Try different openings until you are satisfied you have found the right one. It might encourage you to know that at least half of the scene openings I write are eventually replaced with completely different ones.

Instant Workshop:
Starting a Scene

"Put down that phone!"

What does that line mean? I have no idea. I just thought of it four seconds ago as I was beginning to write this. I was going to start with a different approach, but then that line popped into my mind. Most of the scenes I've written have started this way. I see something or hear something or almost say something—and that becomes the opening of my next scene. It's not as random as it sounds because I'm always on the lookout for a good opening line. What I like about the line above is that it raises so many questions: (1) Who's talking? (2) Who's picked up the phone? (3) Why does the speaker want her to put it down? (4) What was she going to say into the phone? Next, I start wondering what would happen if I tweaked it a little by adding words: "Please put that phone down!" Or "Put that damned phone down!" Each word slightly alters the tone and urgency of the line. This is the fun part of writing—playing with words.

On the first day of my novel writing class, I sometimes tell the students to write an opening sentence that guarantees the reader will want to read the rest of the paragraph. When they are done, we read them aloud and discuss which ones grab our interest the most. Then I have them write the rest of the paragraph. One semester I sat down with them and wrote my own paragraph, just to see how effective the exercise was. The result was that I was so intrigued by my paragraph and by the questions that it brought up that I had to write more. Eventually that single paragraph became the novel *The Joker and the Thief.*

The secret of a good opening is that it must compel the writer as much as the reader. To do this you should think of opening lines as a separate entity from the scene itself. For example, you want to start a scene at a diner counter. The protagonist has to place an order with the waitress because this is their first meeting, which will form a key relationship to the story. What should the first line of the scene be? Yes, we could go with one of the following traditional openings:

> *Bill walked into the diner, sat at the counter and scanned the menu for something not too greasy.*

There's nothing wrong with that and sometimes that straightforward approach is best for a particular scene, but, in general, I prefer an opening that resonates with more mystery. The following opening line starts the scene off with momentum and edginess:

> *"Someone's sitting there," the man in the uniform said as Bill started to straddle the stool.*

How will Bill respond to this line? Will he be angry? What was the tone of the line? What kind of uniform is the man wearing? *What will Bill do next?*

That is the key element of an opening line: It forces the reader to wonder what will happen next. Here's your challenge. Take the above opening scene and write the next three sentences. Do the exercise three times: first, with a menacing tone; second, with a comedic tone; and third, with combination of comedy and menace.

❈ 3 ❈

SIZE-WISE: DETERMINING SCENE LENGTH

> *"I want to give the audience a hint of a scene. No more than that. Give them too much and they won't contribute anything themselves. Give them just a suggestion and you get them working with you."*
>
> Orson Welles

Beginning writers have a tendency to make their scenes either too long or too short. This is perfectly normal, just as a novice basketball player will at first throw the ball too hard, banging it off the backboard, or too soft, clanging it off the front rim. You must also find your range because either too short or long will damage the story. Too-long scenes destroy pace and momentum while too-short scenes prevent the reader from getting involved. As with the basketball player, finding the right range is a matter of practicing until you develop a "feel" for it.

The appropriate length of a scene can be determined the same way you determine the proper length of a lecture on personal hygiene to a five year old: as long as he's still paying attention *and not one second longer*. The unknown element in this equation is the length of the child's attention span, but that is often directly related to just how good a lecturer you are. Do you just wag your finger in his face and say, "Washing your hands helps kill unsanitary germs"? Or do you make it fun by telling a story that includes the washcloth and soap as characters, and acting out all of the parts to drive home your point? The wagging finger may take only a few seconds, but chances are that scene is too long; the storytelling may take fifteen minutes, but it could be too short. Similarly, the best length for a scene has nothing to do with the number of words or pages. Rather, length is determined by the *purpose* of the scene and its *position* among other scenes.

Determining Purpose

Chapter one discusses the various purposes of a scene. In this chapter, we'll examine how long a scene should be in relation to that purpose. For example, if a scene's purpose is to give the reader background about a character's childhood, should it be long or short? First, we must clarify that the terms "long" and "short" are relative to the length of the other scenes around it. If the story in question is a novel, then long might be twenty pages and short might be two pages. But if we're dealing with a twenty-page short story, long might be two pages and short might be two paragraphs.

Nothing about writing is exact, which is why it's an art, not a science. Although the best length of a scene depends on its purpose, there's no rule that any particular purpose should be a specific length. The importance of the scene is not a guide either. Sometimes the most crucial scene in a story may be the shortest to give it the most impact. Therefore, when we discuss length, don't think of pages; think of attention span. Specifically, "long" is when the reader's attention wanders and he either wants to skip ahead or stop reading. "Short" is when the reader feels frustrated because he didn't experience the scene so much as get a synopsis of events. Instead of laying down hard-and-fast rules, I'm just going to present a few general principles regarding purpose and length.

When to Go Short

✤ **Information dumps: plot.** Scenes that function solely to explain the plot should be the shortest. Often writers mistakenly make these the longest because they are so concerned that the reader get every last shred of information. This is especially true in mystery, suspense and science fiction stories. When it's important to deliver plot information, try to do so in a scene that appears to have a different purpose, thereby misdirecting the reader (see chapter one regarding misdirection). Also, it's not important to explain everything to the smallest detail; it's enough to explain the main points and imply the rest. A film like *The Matrix* will always have holes in the plot because of the complexity of the world it has created. But if the main issues are all resolved, the reader will be so caught up in them that you don't want to sacrifice his involvement for the sake of explaining the less important plot details.

- **Information dumps: technical.** Scenes that involve technical information should remain short. For example, one of my students was writing a novel that involved sailing a yacht. This author had great expertise about sailing, so he included page after page of description about the technical aspects of sailing. The workshop reaction to these scenes was the same as always: There was so much technical information that the reader no longer cared about what was happening to the characters. However, there was another student in the same class who was also an expert sailor and writing a novel involving a lot of sailing. The reaction to his sailing scenes was enthusiastic because the reader got just enough information to accept the realism of the scene, but not so much as to be numbing. The purpose of the scene was to make the sailing realistic, which only required a few lines here and there to make the reader a believer. Remember, these novels weren't about sailing. They were about the people involved in sailing. Tom Clancy aside, lengthy technobabble often puts the reader to sleep.

- **Scenic descriptions.** Scenes focusing on descriptions of the scenery, land or weather should remain short. Their power lies with giving the reader an impression, not smothering him with excessive detail. To elaborate on every aspect of the scenery seems as if you are intruding into the story to demonstrate your writing ability. Sometimes you can convey the atmosphere by describing one aspect of the setting. For example, to show that the desert is bleak and dangerous yet intrinsically beautiful, you might describe a single desert plant, detailing every botanical aspect of the plant, how it gets water and how it survives. One paragraph like that will establish "author authority" (the reader's faith that you know what you're talking about) as well as fulfill the purpose of the scene: describing the desert.

✤ **Erotic versus sex.** Erotic scenes should remain short, not out of any modesty but because lengthy scenes can suddenly become comical. Eroticism is merely a matter of body parts interacting in a rush of passion. And, like most things involving a burst of passion, the actions may seem silly if you are given time to reflect. Say someone cuts you off while you're driving. You may feel a rush of anger and speed up to honk, yell or gesture at them. At the moment it's happening (or you're describing it in a story), it can be emotionally intense. But if you keep chasing them for twenty minutes, it seems foolish and pathetic. However, sex scenes (as opposed to merely erotic scenes) designed to show the nature of the relationship can be much longer. Now the scene can include the couple before and after sex, even stopping during sex to take out the dog or answer the phone. (For more details, see chapter twelve.)

When to Go Long

✤ **Conversation.** Scenes that can afford to be longer are scenes that contain conversation. Conversation differs from mere dialogue in that people aren't just talking to convey information, threaten each other or argue. Instead, they are engaged in a discussion that is designed to reveal character. Elmore Leonard is excellent at allowing his characters to talk, seemingly about nothing sometimes. When the scene is over, the reader has a satisfied feeling that he knows these characters on a deeper level and, therefore, cares more about what happens to them. But be careful: Not all dialogue is worthwhile. Writers sometimes include rambling conversations about mundane things because they think it's realistic. In writing terms, "realistic" refers to seeming to be real without actually being real. Most of what people talk about isn't worth repeating, so good dialogue gives the flavor of authenticity by distilling conversation (basically, removing the boring parts). Sometimes everyday conversations are what give a story its energy and establish its characters. The opening scene in the film *Reservoir Dogs* is a perfect example. Several anonymous, tough-looking men are sitting around a restaurant table discussing the meaning of the lyrics to Madonna's "Like a Virgin," and the pros and cons of tipping. This goes on for several minutes without telling the audience who they are or what they're up to. But the conversation is riveting because it is amusing and reveals who each of the characters is. The audience cares more about the men because they had breakfast with them and laughed at their absurd opinions. When the audience realizes the men are all criminals, they already have a certain affection, or at least interest, in them.

- ✤ **Emotional**. Beginning writers often cut their emotional scenes too short, taking the scene right to the point where things get heated and then ending with some faux cliff-hanging line or witty zinger. This shows television's influence where a scene is written to its emotional apex and then cut for a commercial break. When the show comes back, the emotional moment is over and we just see the results of the emotional outburst. However, in real life, the heart of such a scene usually takes place after the point where they cut. Think of your own life. Have you ever had an emotional argument with someone? If you have, you realize that the discussion doesn't end when someone gets in a good line, nor does it usually end at the height of the emotion. Instead, people run out of things to say, they get frustrated, they get weary, they change their minds. This is the messy part of the conversation, the part people don't want to live through and weak writers avoid writing. They'd rather have someone slam the door and leave. Scene over. Next time, keep writing the scene. Stay with the characters so the reader can see what they are made of.
- ✤ **Suspense**. The root of suspense is "suspend." That means you don't rush right in and reveal everything. You tantalize the reader by dangling the scene's climax just out of reach (see chapter ten). Suspense isn't just about chasing people through the streets trying to kill them. It can occur in any kind of scene. For example, you are writing about a couple sitting in a restaurant. The man asks the woman to marry him. Suddenly, the waiter appears: "Are you ready

to order?" "Later," the man says, trying to get rid of him. "Let me tell you the specials," the waiter persists. In this way, you've "suspended" allowing the woman to answer, creating suspense.

Locating Position

Effective scene placement follows the same basic rules as visual arts: Putting contrasting elements next to each other tends to emphasize each work; putting similar elements next to each other tends to blend them together. Therefore, try not to put similar scenes next to each other. Instead, if you have a long conversation scene, put a short descriptive scene after it. Recently in my novel workshop class, a writer submitted two chapters of his suspense novel. The writer is not a beginner; he has published a dozen short stories and his first novel is due out next year. The chapters were each excellent by themselves, but because they were both explanatory, placing them beside each other had the effect of making the second chapter seem long-winded and repetitive. However, when he placed a transitionary chapter between them, the second chapter became more interesting and involving.

Sometimes writers think that if they put all of the action scenes in a row, the story is more exciting. Actually, the opposite often happens. The reader becomes numbed by the repetition. He can't maintain a breathlessness throughout scene after scene and needs a break in between to catch his breath. In *Saving Private Ryan*, the opening battle scene is followed by a calm scene, allowing the characters—and the audience—to recharge their emotional batteries. In fact, the entire film progresses this way: battle scene, calm scene, battle scene, calm scene. Many of the "calm" scenes are memorable because of their positioning. (For help on how to determine scene positioning, see chapter fourteen.)

Of course, this is merely a rule of thumb. Some writers may produce entire stories in which each scene is the same kind and length. Nicholson Baker's novel *Vox* is a phone conversation between two anonymous people. The contrasting scenes in such a story do not depend on external techniques such as setting and description, but rather on the contrast of emotional and intellectual revelations. In one scene, the characters may discuss their opinions about books; in the next, they may reveal deeper emotional secrets. The principle of positioning contrasts still holds true, only the type has changed. Even this book has had chapters and sections within chapters moved around to provide a better contrast of information.

Final Word

The most important thing to remember is that *you don't have to determine the length right away.* When you first begin writing a scene, just write. Don't think about length at all. The real work on determining proper size will come after you've finished a draft of the scene.

About ten years ago I wrote a novel called *Brainwave*. My agent sent it out twice, and both times it was rejected. This was not unusual. Sometimes it took twenty or more rejections before one of my novels was sold, sometimes a novel was bought right away and sometimes I'd sell a novel based on its outline. What was unusual this time was that I asked my agent to stop sending out the book. I felt that there was something wrong with it, but I just hadn't figured out what it was yet. I told her I'd fix it and we'd send it out again. A couple of years passed. I got involved in writing a series of novels and never seemed to get around to *Brainwave*. Impatient, my agent sent it out without telling me and almost immediately we got an offer from a publisher. When I spoke to the editor, she gave me some minor suggestions, then closed with, "There's something that needs to be done to the book, I'm not sure what." There was just something about this book that perplexed both of us. So I plopped the 450 pages of manuscript down and began reading. It quickly became evident what was wrong. Many of the scenes needed trimming, some only a little, some entirely out of existence. I went through that book cutting whole pages and yanking entire chapters. By the time I was finished, I'd cut over a hundred pages, which was a quarter of the book, and that made all the difference. The book now read smoothly with a more urgent pace. I sent it back to the editor and she loved it.

Instant Workshop:
Find the Hot Spot

Every scene has a "hot spot," the moment that the rest of the scene is built around. One way to determine the best length for a scene is to locate that moment and draw a box around it. Then read backward from there. Read the previous paragraph and ask yourself whether or not it (or all of the sentences in it) contributes to that hot spot. Underline any that are suspicious. Then read the paragraph before that one and repeat the process. By altering the traditional linear reading, you get a more objective perspective of each line and are able to cut those that interfere.

✠ 4 ✠

HE SAID, SHE SAID:
DECIDING ON
POINT OF VIEW

"There was a story I wrote...when I was 21, about the death of my grandfather, and...my father as he stood by my grandfather in an old age home. It was all from the point of view of thirteen-year-old me. It failed, it was no good.... So I wrote the story at least once a year, every year...until I was thirty years old. I was old enough to be a father by then, and I finally wrote the story from the point of view of the father instead of the child. ...It worked."

Frederick Busch
author of *Closing Arguments*

"Point of view may be the single most important choice a writer makes.... Point of view offers the controlling framework that shapes any fiction and determines its dimensions."

Alyce Miller
author of *Stopping for Green Lights*

Just as the term implies, *point of view* refers to whose eyes the reader is looking through when observing the events in a scene. For example, you want to write a scene at a basketball game. Do you tell the story from the point of view of one of the players? A referee? A cheerleader? A parent of one of the players? A coach? A kid who's been kicked off the team? Doesn't sound like that big of a deal, does it? Just pick one and get on with the story. But each point of view brings with it advantages and disadvantages, so selecting the proper one can completely change how the reader experiences the scene.

The Japanese film *Rashomon* (as well as a clever episode of *thirtysomething*) is famous for its technique of portraying the same event over and over, but each time it is told from a different character's perspective. As we repeatedly view the same scene, we come to see how each person interprets what he or she sees and experiences. It's the same as when you and a friend discuss something you did together, only each of you has a different version of what happened. Your differing versions reveal more about each of you—how you view events, what you think is important to remember and so on—than it does about what "really" happened. In that same way, point of view is crucial not only in telling about plot events, but in revealing character and making us *care* about those events.

Point of View Options: Who Saw What

The first thing you have to decide is who's telling the story. The narrator is usually the character whom the events are happening to—that is, the person who has the most to win or lose. However, sometimes it's better to have someone else tell the story because it allows for more suspense about the plot or more character development (discussed in chapter two under "The Buddy System"). And sometimes the events affect a lot of different people, so you may want to have multiple narrators, each with his or her own unique point of view.

There are three basic categories of point of view: *first-person, second-person* and *third-person*. Each has advantages, disadvantages and variations that work better with some stories while not at all with others.

FIRST-PERSON POINT OF VIEW: I, ME, MY

Description. If the narrator is using personal pronouns such as "I," "me" and "my," then it is a first-person point of view.

Advantages. This is probably the most popular point of view among beginning writers, although it's a favorite of writers of all levels. The reason for its popularity is its confessional tone. "Let's face it, first person seduces," says writer Alyce Miller. "It may start with little more than a whisper in the ear:

'Psst. Come closer, I'm within you.'" The intimacy of the "I" immediately makes the reader feel like she has a friend who's going to share some juicy personal experience. It's like reading someone else's diary. For instance, what advantages does the reader get from the following passage being in first-person point of view?

> *I walked into the university classroom and looked for an open seat. Stepping over the fake vomit someone had placed in the doorway, I hurried to the seat farthest from the teacher's desk, yet with an unobstructed path to the bathroom. This has been my preferred seat location since fifth grade. Before that I had always sat in the first row, directly in front of the teacher, always the first to raise my hand to answer a question or volunteer to run an errand. But that year Mr. Farley, the new math teacher, began teasing me about the dark hairs sprouting on my legs. (Mother refused to allow me to shave them because it was "frivolous female vanity.") I'd had kind of a crush on Mr. Farley, probably because he was young and had once been a local high school basketball hero. Anyway, one day he'd said something like, "I see you've been fertilizing your legs again, Kyra. When's harvest time?" It wasn't even that funny but everyone laughed and for some reason I got so embarrassed that I peed myself without even knowing it. After that, if I couldn't sit in the back row, I wouldn't take a class. Even though my grades dropped a little because of the move, it was a small price to pay for anonymity.*

You'll notice that the narrator immediately shares a traumatically embarrassing moment with the reader, the kind of moment she probably would only tell her closest friend. This creates an instant bond, a personal relationship that the reader feels some commitment to. The reader also learns something about what's important to the narrator: She'd rather have lower grades than risk embarrassment, even eight years later as a college student. And the reader gets a sense of her upbringing: Her mother had strong views about what a woman should do ("frivolous female vanity"), which creates a personal conflict that the reader expects to hear more about, thereby introducing a suspense hook. There's even the subtle moment when she steps over the fake vomit. Since she doesn't comment on it, it reveals something about her: She could have thought that it was stupid or funny or both. But the fact that she doesn't comment at all tells the reader she's much more focused on getting the perfect reclusive seat, which enhances her desperation and fear of the classroom setting.

Another advantage with first-person point of view is that the reader gets to experience events with more immediacy and impact: "I turned the corner and smacked right into two women carrying bags of groceries." She "feels" physical sensation of colliding and falling as it's happening to the character. However, it doesn't have to be an action. It can also be an emotional revelation: "Dad squeezed my arm and said, 'There's nothing you can do, Kyra. Your mother and I are already divorced.'" Here the reader experiences the shocking surprise as it's happening. True, in both cases, the same events could be experienced in second- or third-person points of view, but in first-person point of view, they are more intimate and have more emotional impact.

This immediacy is why it is such a popular choice among hard-boiled detective novels including such classic examples as those written by Raymond Chandler, Robert Parker, Mickey Spillane and Ross MacDonald. Such works depend on the reader caring about who is murdering whom. But why should the reader care any more than she cares about it in real life, except as a media sideshow curiosity? If she cares about the detective's safety, the stakes have been boosted and the case becomes more important to her. She cares about the detective because, through the use of first-person point of view, he has become her buddy.

Dangers. The strength is also the weakness. The intimacy of the narrator sharing thoughts with the reader is often abused by beginning writers. They don't know when to shut up. Every thought, pet peeve, observation and opinion is crammed into the story until there's no room for plot. It's like having a dinner guest who stays too long, refusing to leave long after you've yawned in his face. He just sits there munching pretzels and spouting opinions that only he finds amusing or interesting. While it's true that what makes the first-person point of view so charming and involving is the cornucopia of thoughts, opinions, observations and peeves, it's also true that you can overdo it. Always ask yourself if the asides enhance the characterization or detract from it. Don't be afraid to cut passages, no matter how wry or witty, and save them for later in the story or for another story altogether. Most writers have files of favorite passages they've cut from various stories, but hope to use in another one.

Variations. In Joseph Conrad's novella, *The Heart of Darkness*, the first-person narrator is *not* the one the events happened to. In fact, he happens upon the character of Marlow, who proceeds to tell the entire story of his seeking the elusive Kurtz. What's interesting is that the story is about Kurtz's moral corruption. Yet Kurtz's story is told by Marlow because he's an innocent who's in for some major shocks when he finally discovers Kurtz. The impact then is to experience Marlow's reaction to Kurtz, which is more powerful in first-person point of view. Then why have Marlow tell a different first-person point of view narrator the story? Why not just tell the story from Marlow's point of view and be done with it? Because the reader has the additional contrast of seeing right from the beginning how much Marlow has been changed by the events he's about to tell her. This adds suspense about what he's going to say. The reader can't help but lean a little closer. The same technique is used in the film, *The Man Who Would Be King*, based on a story by Rudyard Kipling. In the film, Kipling (Christopher Plummer) is visited by a hunched man in rags whose face is horribly scarred. Half-blind and barely able to walk, the man (Michael Caine) tells Kipling they are old friends. When Kipling realizes who it is, he is horrified. Only a year ago, this man stood before him a young, energetic, tough soldier. The story then is a flashback narrative of Caine's adventures with his pal Danny (Sean Connery). Both stories use a double first-person point of view. The first narrator represents us, the audience, who will be shocked by what we hear. The second narrator, to whom the adventure actually happened, also represents the audience in that we identify with that character as we experience everything through his rational eyes. But both stories are really about the third character—Kurtz and Danny—who get lost in their adventures, having abandoned rationality to passion. It's a tricky but highly effective narrative technique. And since we already know the disastrous results their adventures had on their lives, we want to know what went wrong. This increases the stakes and our involvement.

Another variation is to have a story told from several different first-person points of view. Each scene or chapter is still from the "I" point of view, but it's a different "I" each time. This allows the reader to maintain that confessional relationship but with more than one character. Since the reader shares so many secret thoughts, the plot stakes are multiplied by the number of narrators. There's more suspense about how all of the narrators will be affected by whatever happens. The disadvantage is that the reader's commitment to any one individual can be diluted, which lowers the emotional stakes.

SECOND-PERSON POINT OF VIEW: YOU, YOU, YOU

Description. If the narrator is using the personal pronoun "you," then it is a second-person point of view. This is extremely rare.

Advantages. The second-person point of view creates a unique tone in a story—a removed, ironic tone that hints at an underlying bitterness. Probably the most famous recent example of this point of view is Jay McInerney's novel, *Bright Lights, Big City*, which begins as follows:

> *You are not the kind of guy who would be at a place like this at this time of morning. But here you are, and you cannot say that the terrain is entirely unfamiliar, although the details are fuzzy.*

Basically, the second-person point of view acts as a kind of chiding conscience, the moral superego showing the main character what his life has become. There's usually a hint of condemnation in this point of view, a "how-have-you-sunk-so-low?" attitude. For example, Lorrie Moore, in her brilliant collection of stories *Self-Help*, uses this point of view in several of her stories:

> *First try to be something else, anything else. A movie star/astronaut. A movie star/missionary. A movie star/kindergarten*

> *teacher. President of the world. Fail miserably. It is best if you*
> *fail at an early age—say, fourteen. Early, critical disillusion-*
> *ment is necessary so that at fifteen you can write long haiku se-*
> *quences about thwarted desire.*
>
> from *"How to Become a Writer"*

> *Meet in expensive beige raincoats, on a pea-soupy night. Like*
> *a detective movie. First, stand in front of Florsheim's Fifty-*
> *seventh Street window, press your face close to the glass, watch*
> *the fake velvet Hummels inside revolving around the wing tips;*
> *some white shoes, like your father wears, are propped up with*
> *garlands on a small mound of chemical snow. All the stores*
> *have closed. You can see your breath on the glass. Draw a peace*
> *sign. You are waiting for a bus.*
>
> from *"How to Be an Other Woman"*

Each of these passages has a dry, humorous wit, but we can also see the narrator sadly hiding behind the "you" of the second-person point of view. This gives each passage an extra poignancy, as if someone were asking you for personal advice, but clumsily pretending it was for a friend.

Dangers. We don't see this used too often because it's more difficult for the reader to get involved than with the other points of view. One reason is that its rarity makes it less familiar, but more important is that its attraction to the writer—the fact that it allows a remoteness, which creates a darker tone—is what repels many readers. They don't mind dark tones, but they don‘t want to be so far removed from the characters who are experiencing that darkness. This is why second-person point of view is mostly used in literary fiction and, even then, usually in short stories.

THIRD-PERSON POINT OF VIEW: HE, SHE, THEY

Description. If the narration involves the personal pronouns "he," "she" or "they," then it is a third-person point of view. There are two basic classifications of third-person point of view: *omniscient* and *limited omniscient*.

Advantages. The godlike omniscient point of view allows the reader to move around from character to character, and even in time and space. For instance, the reader could experience an argument from the point of view of the character in-stigating the argument and, in the very next sentence, could be in the point of view of the character on the receiving end.

> *Sarah Leary pulled into her driveway and saw the neighbor's boy Timothy raking leaves, sloppily and with a grudging frown, the way he did everything. She felt the anger literally rising in her, heating her chest, then her neck, finally flushing through her face. As she jumped out of the car, the cool October air stung her burning skin.*
>
> *"Timothy! Come here, right now!" she hollered.*
>
> *Timothy's look of innocence was automatic, practiced through many similar scenes that always began with the shout-ing of his name. It was a reflex that would come in handy years later during his five-year prison term for holding up a liquor store. He didn't move right away, trying to remember what ex-actly he might have done to Mrs. Leary or her dweeby little brat, Stanley.*

The first paragraph presents Sarah Leary's point of view: anger at Timothy. The second paragraph presents Timothy's point of view: defensiveness and cunning. This multiple point of view adds richness to a scene, allowing us to experience the events through more than one person's eyes. Notice the line about Timothy's eventual prison term; this point of view allows the writer to reveal future information about a character that will affect how the reader views the character during the scene. The reader now knows that Timothy isn't going to suddenly see the error of his delinquent ways. You might think knowing this would remove suspense about what he may do in this scene; actually, it creates even more suspense. Now the reader knows that whatever he does, it will not be good, and she anticipates this. This technique of telling the eventual fate of characters was used to great advantage by John Irving in his novel, *The World According to Garp.*

The limited omniscient point of view differs in that it lim-its what the reader sees to the perspective of one person at a time. She sees the events from the viewpoint of only one char-acter within a scene, chapter or even the whole story or novel.

The reader is exposed to only that one character's thoughts, reactions, vision. However, many books that use limited omniscience still alternate points of view from chapter to chapter. This technique is especially popular in longer suspense novels, such as Stephen King's *The Stand* and *Firestarter*, and my own suspense thrillers *Masked Dog* and *The Remington Factor*. When I started each of those novels, I deliberately selected the third-person limited omniscient point of view so I could move back and forth between the villain and the hero—as well as other secondary characters—and create more suspense. Since both the reader and I knew what the villain's and the hero's plans were, I could write a scene from the villain's point of view in which something happens to cause him to change his plan, destroying the hero's plan and putting him in grave danger. Then I could go back to the unknowing hero's point of view and have him go through with his now-doomed plan. But in this scene, I could emphasize the likable aspects of his character to increase the reader's emotional involvement with him.

Suspense master Alfred Hitchcock once said that the key to suspense is showing the audience the bomb planted under the desk, the clock ticking and a person we like sitting at the desk, oblivious. To make us see the bomb, we go into the point of view of the person planting it, setting the clock. To make us like the person at the desk, we go into her point of view, understanding that she is sitting at that desk because she's grading student papers. She has a date and really should leave, but she loves her students so much that she agreed to meet with little Sally after class to help her with her math. Oops, here comes Sally now, pulling up a little chair beside the desk with the bomb. Will teacher and Sally finish in time?

Dangers. Too many points of view can dilute tension. If the reader gets too many characters' backgrounds, too many people plotting and scheming and wanting, she gets a bit confused and withdraws her emotional commitment to what's going on so she can concentrate on following the plot complications. When Stephen King's *The Stand* was first published, it had been drastically edited to eliminate some of what the editor thought were these same problems. Only years later, when the novel had become a cult classic, was the original uncut version released. Some reviewers subsequently agreed with the slimmer first edition. In fact, some reviewers thought the original edited version needed to be cut as well.

Nothing But the Truth

Once you've chosen among the narrative options listed above, you have another decision to make: Will your narrator be reliable or unreliable? It's not as simple as deciding whether or not they'll be honest. It's more subtle than that. A narrator can be telling the reader the truth—as he sees it—yet still not be telling the reader what she sees is really the truth. Holden Caulfield in *The Catcher in the Rye* tells the reader the way he sees the world. It's the truth, but it's *Holden's* truth. His reality. The author wants the reader to see that Holden doesn't see the world accurately; that's his whole problem. His vision of the world has been distorted by the unrealistic, God-in-His-heaven, Hollywood happy-ending vision that he's been raised on, and by the harsh reality of an indifferent universe that allowed his innocent and loving younger brother to die of leukemia. In fact, the novel is Holden's journey to coming to his own vision, which is a balance of the two. The reason this novel is so effective is that it uses his humorous and compassionate first-person point of view to make the reader like and care for him, while allowing her to see the contradictions in his observations that he can't see. Not only does the reader care for him, but she worries over him because she can see why he is suffering even if he can't, and knows that he is heading for a great fall.

The unreliable narrator is a major device in literature (see the section on "Character Description" in chapter two). Joyce Carol Oates's story "Naked" is about a woman out on a jog who is attacked by a group of young children, stripped naked and left to find her way home. But the story isn't about the horror of the event, which would reduce it to merely a plot-driven story. Instead, Oates has taken a true-life incident (the "wilding" of the woman known as the Central Park Jogger) and looked for a truth beneath the incident itself. She could have focused the story on illuminating the evils of a society that produces such children, but that would have been obvious and preachy. Instead, the incident is used as a vehicle to strip away the woman's illusions and misperceptions about her own life, eventually leaving her "naked" of the rationalizations that have allowed her to hide from her true self. The only way this story can convey this insight is by creating a character who tells the reader about herself throughout the story, only to have the reader realize that she has no idea who she really is. At one point, she describes her own sobbing after the attack as at least not being hysterical, "for she was not a hysterically inclined woman; she was a woman who might quell hysteria in others." But immediately after telling the reader this, she decides not to seek the help of two men who are jogging nearby. She decides to sneak home—naked—through several blocks of underbrush rather than have people think of her as less than competent. The reader realizes that she is imprisoned by how others might view her. Here are two passages from the story that illustrate how to show an unreliable narrator:

> *She was by nature and training an unfailingly friendly woman; she practiced friendliness as a musician practices an instrument, and with as unquestioned a devotion.*

The first excerpt shows how little insight she has into herself: To practice friendliness is not the same as actually being friendly; it is merely an imitation.

> *She had had her children after all as she'd determined to have them. She would not have had two children had she not wanted them, for one would have done. Two was incontestable proof.*

The second excerpt is interesting because Oates didn't have it in early drafts of the story. She added it later, obviously because she wanted to emphasize how far this woman would go to fit in. Her explanation of why she had two children—because now others would know for sure that she chose to have children—reveals just how deeply mired in denial she is.

Gender, Age and Race:
The World According to—Whomever You Want
Aside from specific first-, second- and third-person points of

view, there is always the question of who the narrator should be. What will the narrator's gender, age and race be? Beginning writers may feel more comfortable writing from a point of view that mirrors their own. I certainly did when I started writing. My first six novels were all in the first-person point of view, the narrator being nothing more than a much more interesting version of me. He had my sense of humor, my opinions, my outlook on life. Sometimes they were exaggerated for effect, but basically he was my clone. However, a writer should never feel restricted to that. If you want to write from the point of view of someone who is a different age, gender, race or even species than you, do it.

A few years ago, a writer named Danny Santiago wrote a novel (*Famous All Over Town*) from the point of view of a young Latino boy. The book won rave reviews and received accolades from the Latin community. However, when it was revealed the novel had actually been written by an elderly Caucasian man, there were some who were angry. The same outcry happened several decades ago when acclaimed novelist William Styron wrote the best-selling *The Confessions of Nat Turner* from the point of view of a black man. More recently, Wally Lamb wrote the best-seller and Oprah Book Club selection *She's Come Undone* from a woman's point of view. (I have also written several mainstream novels from women's points of view under my pseudonym, Laramie Dunaway.) Not to mention the dozens of science fiction novels written from the point of view of aliens, or Richard Adams's *Watership Down*, which is from the point of view of rabbits. There are many examples of people writing from points of view diametrically opposite of their own lives and achieving great success doing so. More importantly, think of all the wonderful stories that we wouldn't have if writers limited themselves to writing from points of view that only matched their own lives. We'd be without works from *Peter Pan* to *The Wizard of Oz* to *Gone With the Wind*.

Final Word

As with everything in writing, don't be afraid to experiment. Remember that there is no rule that you have to have the same point of view throughout a story or novel. Some novels will alternate chapters between first-person and third-person point of view. Try a passage in one point of view, then rewrite it in another. Dashiell Hammett wrote the original *The Thin Man* novel from the point of view of his popular Continental Op character, only to scrap it after ninety pages and begin anew with different characters, Nick and Nora Charles. Sometimes I will write five or six chapters of a novel in first person, only to go back and rewrite it from the third-person point of view and vice-versa. Why? Just to see how it feels, how it sounds, which way is more authentic or involving and, most crucial, which would be the most fun for me to write.

❊ 5 ❊
YOU ARE HERE:
USING SETTING

"The famous rules, which the French call Des Trois Unitez, *or, the Three Unities, which ought to be observed in every regular play; namely, of Time, Place, and Action."*

John Dryden

"Hammett took murder out of the parlor and put it in the alley where it belongs."

Raymond Chandler

The *setting* is the location where the events of the scene take place. This could be in a room, park, car, pool hall, the White House—a thousand different places. Beginning writers are sometimes lax in taking advantage of this key element because they too often focus on the more dynamic elements of plot, character and dialogue. While it's true that those elements are crucial to the success of the story, it's also true that selecting the right setting can significantly enhance the story's impact. Choosing where a scene takes place can add thematic dimension or suspense (for an example, see "What Makes a Scene Memorable?" in chapter one). While working on my own novels, I have often rewritten scenes that seemed flat by transporting them to an entirely new setting. This suddenly made the scene more exciting, intense or comical, depending upon what I was trying to achieve.

Filmmaker Orson Welles was especially masterful in using setting to heighten all of the elements of his films. In *The Lady From Shanghai*, the lovers meet secretly at a public aquarium. As they embrace in the semidarkness, sensually illuminated by the enormous fish tanks, their barely pent passion is enhanced. Plus, there is also the danger of exposure because they're in a public place, as we see when a group of school children giggle after discovering the couple kissing. How much different the scene would have been if it had been set in a restaurant over nachos. Later in the film, Welles has all of the principal characters shooting at each other in a funhouse mirror building (a scene duplicated in other movies such as Bruce Lee's *Enter the Dragon* and Woody Allen's *Manhattan Murder Mystery*). Not only does this create suspense as they mistakenly shoot at the various mirrors, but it emphasizes the thematic motif of conniving people who deliberately present deceptive personas to each other. Finally, in Welles's *The Third Man*, the climactic chase through the dark confines of the Vienna sewer system allows for much more excitement than it would have had it taken place out on the open streets.

A good way to understand the importance of setting is to list a few of your favorite story, novel and film scenes, and imagine them set elsewhere.

How Much Setting Description Is Enough?

The answer is simple: enough to achieve your goal, but not so much as to detract from the other elements of the scene. Yes, I know that's a bit ambiguous, but that's because every scene has a *dominating purpose*: to give plot information, to develop character, to create suspense, etc. Once you decide what that dominant purpose is, all of the other elements of the scene must be subordinate to it. Sometimes the dominant purpose of the scene is to establish setting, in which case more time should be spent doing just that.

Beginning writers are notorious for two errors concerning setting: (1) overdescribing and (2) clumping. *Overdescribing* is tempting because scene description is an opportunity to show off your prose skills through elaborate metaphor-strewn descriptions. *Resist the temptation.* It is indeed an opportunity to demonstrate prose style virtuosity, but the power of the description comes from the impact of having just enough rather than diluting it with too much. You should use all the metaphoric and word-choice skills you have, just use them sparingly. If you want to show us a filthy, disgusting alley, don't feel compelled to drag us through each slimy puddle, toss us into an overflowing trash dumpster, then rub our noses in the dried vomit. As with most things in life, sometimes less is more. Use one metaphor, one adjective, one defining characteristic of a room rather than two or three. Think of fiction setting the same way you might a play's set. Most of the time a stage play uses set design to *imply* the larger setting. The false fronts of buildings, even the elaborate interiors may be realistic, but the audience never mistakes them for real. If you want the reader to experience how depressing a hospital ward is, you only have to imply it by describing a few aspects that suggest the larger image:

> *The hallways seemed narrower and darker than other hospitals I'd been in, but that could have been because of the artwork on the walls: oversized prints of small ships being tossed on stormy scenes. As I walked down the hall, the ships seemed to get smaller and the storms more violent. Though I saw no one else in the hall, the constant sound of slippers scuffing across linoleum accompanied me like a harsh ocean wind.*

There is no attempt to describe the antiseptic smells, drab paint jobs, indifferent faces of the staff or defeated expressions of the patients that are usually used. Instead, the sinister artwork on the wall and the unseen shuffling of slippers creates the ominous mood without slowing the pace.

I'll leave the subject of overdescription with some words of advice Anton Chekhov gave a young writer: "Descriptions of nature should be extremely brief and offered by the way, as it were. Give up commonplaces, such as: 'the setting sun, bathing in the waves of the darkening sea, flooded with purple gold,' and so on. Or 'Swallows flying over the surface of the water chirped gaily.' In descriptions of nature one should seize upon minutiae, grouping them so that when, having read the passage, you close your eyes, a picture is formed. For example, you will evoke a moonlit night by writing that on the mill dam the glass fragments of a broken bottle flashed like a bright little star, and that the black shadow of a dog or wolf rolled along like a ball."

Clumping occurs when a writer unloads the entire description in one section of the scene. The momentum of the scene grinds to a halt while the reader must endure paragraph after paragraph of description of the car, scenery, weather and a history of the bugs splatting against the windshield. First, decide whether or not that information is crucial to the scene. Does it enhance the scene or are you just showing off? Second, it is usually better to dole out these descriptive moments throughout a scene, between more active moments. In Elizabeth Tallent's "No One's a Mystery," the eighteen-year-old narrator is riding in a truck with her older, married lover. He's bought her a diary for her birthday and is telling her that life is so predictable, he knows what she will write in it that night:

> *"How do you know?"*
>
> *"I just know," he said. "Like I know I'm going to get meat loaf for supper. It's in the air. Like I know what you'll be writing in that diary."*
>
> *"What will I be writing?" I knelt on my side of the seat and craned around to look at the butterfly of dust printed on my jeans. Outside the window Wyoming was dazzling in the heat. The wheat was fawn and yellow and parted smoothly by the thin dirt road. I could smell the water in the irrigation ditches hidden in the wheat.*

The cleverness of this technique is that first a question is asked ("What will I be writing?") and then the setting description is placed between the question and answer. This insures that the reader is paying more attention to the description because Tallent has heightened his awareness by asking an important question. They are more focused on the setting description. Plus, Tallent has heightened the suspense by delaying the answer. Raymond Carver uses the same technique in "A Small, Good Thing." Ann's eight-year-old son is in the hospital. The doctor keeps assuring her the boy's okay, but she suspects otherwise:

> *"Why doesn't he wake up?" Ann said.*
>
> *The doctor was a handsome, big-shouldered man with a tanned face. He wore a three-piece blue suit, a striped tie, and ivory cuff links. His gray hair was combed along the sides of his head, and he looked as if he had just come from a concert. "He's all right," the doctor said.*

Again, the question is posed, this time by a desperate mother, but the response is withheld while the reader gets a description of the doctor. The description is that of a confident, successful man, a professional whose opinion the mother should listen to—an ironic description since the doctor is wrong and the boy is in grave danger.

That's one technique of placement to avoid clumping. In Tallent's description, there's more going on than just details about the setting. Start with her reference to the dust splotch on the girl's pants as a "butterfly." She uses this word because the girl is a romantic kid who thinks this is the love of her life, even though the guy's telling her it's nothing more than another in a long, mundane string of affairs. The rest of the description of Wyoming is very concise: bright, wheat fields; dirt roads; the smell of irrigation water. It may seem a little desolate to the reader, suggesting why the girl is with him in the first place (limited opportunities), but Tallent's word choices echo the girl's romanticism even here. She calls Wyoming "dazzling" instead of blistering. She uses "fawn" to describe the color. The road parts the wheat field "smoothly." Without overdoing the description, the reader gets a snapshot of the scenery they're driving through, which also defines their existence and choices, but also gets a peek at the kind of girl she is.

To avoid clumping, find the right place in the scene to give the reader the descriptions and, remember, you don't have to give everything at once. As David Guterson, author of *Snow Falling on Cedars* and *East of the Mountains*, advises, "[Y]ou may get bogged down in a sentence that's descriptive detail about landscape, spend a lot of time on it, then realize that the entire paragraph, maybe the entire page, maybe two or three pages of descriptive detail are doing nothing...and it's time to remove them. But there's a lot of satisfaction in tearing away, and allowing something really clear to emerge as a result."

How Does Setting Relate to Pacing?

So far we've discussed techniques for presenting setting descriptions, but how to select that setting is another matter. One aspect to consider is that the choice of setting can control the pace of the story. This can mean one of two possibilities: (1) it controls the pace within a particular scene, or (2) the scene itself is used to control the pace of a larger story or novel. A suspense novel generally involves chasing after someone, but if every scene is a wild chase, the reader will lose interest. So the suspense novel must include sedentary scenes to separate the faster-paced chase scenes. A scene at a Paris café might be followed by a chase scene up the Eiffel Tower, but the effectiveness of the chase is dependent upon the contrast.

Most detective novels follow the same pattern: There's a crime after which the detective must interview a bunch of people to find out who committed the crime. These interviews are there not only to gather information, but also to introduce suspects. The problem each detective novel writer faces is how to make this round of interviews interesting. One way is to hamper the detective. Rex Stout's Nero Wolfe chooses never to leave his home; instead, he sends his sidekick (the first-person narrator) Archie Goodwin to do the legwork. The reader now knows that for the mystery to be solved, the suspects must show up at Wolfe's home, a setting so familiar and comfortable to the reader it's like his own home. Jeffery Deaver's quadriplegic forensic expert in *The Bone Collector* also cannot leave his home, so the settings are a constant juxtapositioning of his bedroom, the crimes in progress and his sidekick who is trying to solve the murders.

Another technique is to make each interview like its own mininovel. The person being interviewed is so compelling that the reader can't take his eyes off the character. In addition to the riveting character, an unusual setting helps misdirect the reader from the fact that he's just following a pattern. For example, it's popular to interview a character at work, which gives the author an opportunity to describe the workplace and the details of the job. Let's say the character trains dolphins for Sea World. The reader gets all sorts of interesting information about how that's done. Of course, this involves research. I once decided to have a suspect pilot a skywriting plane. In order to give the scene as much authentic texture as possible, I went to a local skydiving company and interviewed a pilot. At their core, such scenes are the same: introduce the suspect and give the reader information toward solving the mystery. The author's expertise at characterization and setting are what distinguish the good from the bad.

How Does Setting Relate to Theme?

Sometimes you might select a particular setting just because it's interesting or it helps make the scene more exciting or suspenseful. At other times, setting has a more substantial function than a backdrop for events; it can be a major character in the story. This is especially true in what Hollywood refers to as "fish out of water" stories. In such scenarios, a person leaves the place where they are comfortable and journeys to a place where everything is different. These differences become the core settings of each scene. Examples include *Splash* (mermaid on land), *Witness* (tough cop among peaceful Amish), *Deliverance* (arrogant city boys among reclusive mountain folk), *Next of Kin* (tough hillbilly cop in the big city), *Beverly Hills Cop* (tough Detroit cop in wealthy Beverly Hills), *Coogan's Bluff* (tough Western cop in New York City), *Billy Madison* (immature adult sent back to grade school), *Happy Gilmore* (hockey player on the pro golf tour) and so on. It's highly popular because it allows for instant conflict in the clash of cultures, which, let's face it, is just plain fun. However, this contrast can be used to create a richer thematic layer as well.

Certainly in many works, the nature of the landscape is a major influence on why characters do what they do: the roiling sea in Herman Melville's *Moby Dick* and Stephen Crane's "Open Boat"; the Southwest desert in Barbara Kingsolver's *Animal Dreams*; the rugged West in most Westerns; the dust bowl Midwest in John Steinbeck's *The Grapes of Wrath*; the dense jungle in Joseph Conrad's *The Heart of Darkness* and Paul Theroux's *The Mosquito Coast*. In each of these stories, the setting isn't just a place where the events of the story happen; it is a motivating factor in why people do what they do.

In literature, for example, the sea is often symbolic of the indifference of nature toward humans. On land, humans have more control over their environment and, therefore, base their beliefs about their own role in the universe on this sense of order. But the sea can't be controlled, so once the characters are afloat on the sea, they reexamine their previous beliefs about the universe. This is what happens in *Moby Dick* and "Open Boat," as well as most of the novels by Joseph Conrad. By the way, jungles often symbolize the same loss of control (see the Conrad and Theroux stories mentioned above).

Final Word

As with most aspects of writing, it's not a matter of either one technique or the other. Either I select an interesting setting to pick up the pace or I select one that is more thematic; either I have long passages describing settings or I keep the descriptions short and punchy. Start by writing a scene any way you feel like writing it. Realize that much of the initial writing is you discovering the story and sometimes setting can help in that discovery. E.L. Doctorow had difficulty beginning his critically acclaimed best-seller, *Ragtime,* until he wrote the opening line, "I live in a house that was built in 1906." Although it does not appear in the final draft of the book, he credits that line as being "the embryo of the book: It has the images which got me going."

Instant Workshop:
Choosing Settings

Director John Ford was a pioneer with his Westerns in that he used the actual settings of the West to help audiences experience the rugged and unforgiving environment that helped shape the morals and character of the people exposed to it. His characters weren't just wandering around the backlots of Tarzana pretending to be in Arizona; they were actually there, often dwarfed by the canyons, deserts and pastures where the real people lived and died. It helps when a writer understands the connection between setting, character and plot. Sometimes the setting is just window dressing to add spice to the scene, but the core settings, just like the main sets of a play, carry a greater weight. When choosing settings, fill in the information to the following:

1. Describe the characteristics of the setting:

2. The setting affects the character(s) in the following ways:

3. The setting affects the plot in the following ways:

This can be done both on the grander scale of the general setting of the story (e.g., Orange County, California) and the smaller setting of an individual scene (e.g., a restaurant). Here is a completed example:

1. Describe the characteristics of the setting:

General setting: *Orange County (the setting of T. Jefferson Parker's novel,* Laguna Heat, *among others). A sprawling suburban cluster of many smaller cities that seem to overlap each other, each connected by always-jammed freeways. Includes a large spectrum of socioeconomic classes, from the wealthy socialites of Newport Beach to the surf-and-party beach communities of Huntington Beach to the gang-infested neighborhoods of Santa Ana to the strictly planned communities of Irvine. Also includes one of the largest Vietnamese communities in the country. Every strata of society is here, generally commingling at the supermalls of South Coast Plaza and Fashion Island.*

Specific setting: *Rain Forest restaurant at South Coast Plaza. Theme restaurant with jungle sounds and exotic birds. Always busy, especially with mothers and their children. The entrance is usually filled with dozens of empty strollers. Perfect scene for a heated emotional discussion because the characters might feel restricted about what they can say—and what language they can use—due to all the kids.*

✖ 6 ✖

FOND FAREWELL OR
GOOD RIDDANCE:
ENDING A SCENE

*"Great is the art of beginning, but greater
the art is of ending;
Many a poem is marred by a superfluous
verse."*
Henry Wadsworth Longfellow

The ending of a scene is like a goodnight kiss on a first date: It must project a physical sensation that both comments on the date that just ended and communicates the desirability of any future dates. The lingering mashing of lips and tongues says, "Had a great time. Let's do it again *soon*." The quick peck on the cheek says, "If you call, you'll get my answering machine." I use the word "sensation" because the last lines of a scene— aside from whatever else the author wants to do intellectually—must create a *feeling* in the reader. A feeling of completion about the scene that is ending as well as anticipation urging the reader forward to the next scene. In the final analysis, that's the ending's most important function: *to make the reader satisfied with the scene she just read and to make her want to turn the page.* Any ending that doesn't do that is a bad ending.

Sometimes a really strong scene ending can save an otherwise mediocre scene. It's the same in boxing. In the latter part of his career, Muhammad Ali used to lay back the first two minutes of a round—dance out of the way, counterpunch, rope-a-dope—then in the final minute, he'd unleash a flurry of punches in order to convince the judges he was in control the whole time. Usually it worked. How many times have you gotten to the end of a chapter in a novel and put it aside with every intention of coming back to it, yet you never did? You were never compelled enough by those final lines to drive you forward. And how many times have you watched a bland TV show, telling yourself you'd shut it off at the commercial, when suddenly there'd be some exciting moment right at the end? You then find yourself still sitting there when the commercial is over, wanting to know what will happen next.

The best way to write a strong ending is to think of each scene as a complete story with its own beginning, middle and ending. The ending moments complete the scene and justify its existence by leaving the reader with an emotional or intellectual impact—sometimes both. Because each scene is part of a larger story, the ending of a particular scene is like handing the reader a piece to a jigsaw puzzle, which is their reward for completing the scene. Make no mistake. That's exactly what it is: a reward. When completing the final sentence of a scene, the reader should think, "Ah, that was good. I'd like another," and plunge ahead to the next scene. Not only must the ending of the scene be enjoyable to read, but it should also complete a crucial section of the story-puzzle so that the reader understands the larger puzzle better, compelling her forward to find the next piece.

Basically, there are two types of scene endings: endings that emphasize *plot* or *character*. One type is not intrinsically better than the other; the best writers will have some of each. However, depending on the kind of story you are writing, one type will dominate.

Plot Endings

Genre fiction focuses on the plot endings. Yes, there are many excellent writers whose work transcends the genre into literary fiction, but the fact that they chose to write within a particular genre indicates a preference for the parameters of that genre. They chose it because they like the plot elements. When Simon and Garfunkel first became famous with their blend of folk and rock, an interviewer questioned Paul Simon about the unusually powerful lyrics he wrote. He asked Simon if he wasn't really more of a poet than a songwriter. Simon replied that if he were a poet, he'd write poetry, but he was a songwriter because when it came to choosing words or music in a song, he always sacrificed the words to fit the music. That's how genre writers feel.

For readers, genre fiction is like a roller coaster ride: They know what the ride's going to be like and that's why they buy the ticket. It's the writer's job to provide the best ride possible. One of the key techniques to enhancing the ride is the use of suspenseful scene endings, particularly the *cliff-hanger*. This technique gets its name from the old movie serials that ended each episode with the hero in dire physical peril, such as hanging from a cliff, hand slipping, looking down at a pit filled with (choose one): (a) sharpened stakes, (b) venomous snakes or (c) molten lava. The same technique is still used (as in *Raiders of the Lost Ark*, a homage to those serials) to great effect.

A novel chapter may be composed of many scenes, each with its own ending. Usually if the ending of the chapter itself is a cliff-hanger, the other scene endings won't be cliff-hangers. This avoids stealing any impact from the final surprise. Instead, the other scene endings will concentrate on ratcheting up the suspense elements. The scene may end with one of the characters wondering if she'll ever see her family again, or someone will look around and say, "This doesn't look like the way we came." With each of those lines, the reader's anxiety level is increased. So when the group of travelers is left at the end of the chapter wondering what the hell those creatures are that are running at them from all sides, howling and grunting, their eyes glowing a strange red—she is definitely ready to turn the page. The scene endings leading up to the final cliff-hanger are like whispering into the reader's ear, "Look out, pal. Things just keep getting worse and worse." Though there are many variations, the following examples are two of the most popular types of scene endings that focus on plot: the cliff-hanger ending and the if-I'd-only-known ending.

THE CLIFF-HANGER ENDING

This ending was described above. It is characterized by stopping the scene just as a major action is about to take place. In the following scene, the narrator is a physician whose depressed fiancé has just shown up at her clinic waving a gun. She tries to talk him out of the gun.

TIP

Jump Cuts Plus Cliff-Hangers Equal Suspense

Obviously, part of the power of the cliff-hanger ending is that it whips the reader up to an emotional state that shoves her into the next chapter. However, there's nothing that says your next scene has to be a continuation of the cliff-hanger. Some writers use the reader's heightened curiosity to insert a scene or chapter that may take her to a different location or time, or with different characters (see "The Jump Cut" in chapter two). For example, if a scene ends with a character in great jeopardy, the next scene may be a flashback into that character's youth. Or the next scene may take the reader to different characters altogether. The writer is hoping that the reader's curiosity level is great enough to make her read this chapter with more attention than she might have without the cliff-hanger preceding it. Some suspense novelists alternate cliff-hangers: I end one scene with Mary in her bedroom hearing someone breaking down her front door. The next scene is a flashback to Mary at sixteen, shoplifting from Kmart. The scene ends with a security guard chasing her down the cosmetics aisle. When I go back to continue the story of Mary in her bedroom, the reader is curious about what will happen there, but also wants to know what happened with the security guard.

Notice that the example I used above from my novel, Earth Angel, *ends the first chapter/scene with a cliff-hanger ("That's when the shooting started"). However, the very next scene is* not *the shooting. Instead, it starts like this:*

"I'm hurrying," I said.

That horrible cry again.

"I'm *hurrying*," I repeated, stepping out of my underpants. I reached into the shower, turned on the hot water faucet, and quickly ducked back out before getting splashed.

This scene takes place weeks after the shooting in the clinic. At this point, we see the narrator, Dr. Season Gottlieb, trying to recover from having her life destroyed. But I want the reader to be a little disoriented by the lack of linear narrative; I want them to feel the way she feels. "What is she doing now?" the reader should be asking. "What happened at the clinic?" What she's doing is nursing a sick kitten, a gift from a well-wishing friend following the funeral of Season's fiancé. By showing the results of the shooting first, I'm trying to make the shooting more meaningful than just an action sequence. When I finally describe the shooting in the following scene, the reader isn't focused on the action as much as on the characters. In that way, it's less of a genre scene and more literary (I hope).

> *"Tim," I said softly and took a step toward him. I was crying, though I didn't know when I'd started. "Tim, please." I reached out to hold him, make things better.*
>
> *That's when the shooting started.*
>
> from *Earth Angel* by Raymond Obstfeld

In this next scene, twenty-something Greg Fisher is visiting the former Soviet Union. He gets out of his car at night to look at a war monument. When he makes his way back to his car, it is so dark he can only see his car's headlights.

> *The glare of his headlights blinded him, and he shielded his eyes as he walked in long strides the ten meters back toward his car; one, two, three, four, five—*
>
> *"Russian efficiency," said a voice a few feet to his right.*
>
> *Fisher felt his knees go weak.*
>
> from *The Charm School* by Nelson DeMille

THE IF-I'D-ONLY-KNOWN ENDING

This type of ending is characterized by someone implying that, had they known the events contained on the next page, they might have acted differently. This requires "superior knowledge" (knowledge of the future) on the part of the narrator, whether the narrator is a character in the novel or an omniscient narrator.

In the following scene ending, the narrator is a seventeen-year-old boy whose mother and new husband live in Hawaii. His father, with whom he lives, finally talks him into visiting her.

> *We both laughed and pretty soon I was feeling better about going. If I'd known what was going to happen to me in Hawaii, I wouldn't have been laughing so hard.*
>
> from *The Joker and the Thief* by Raymond Obstfeld

This next scene ending involves a forensic anthropologist who has just examined the dismembered parts of a corpse.

> *...I wouldn't be sleeping in Quebec City this weekend. In fact, as I drove the few short blocks to my condo, I suspected that no*

one would be sleeping much for a long time. As things turned out, I was right. What I couldn't have known then was the full extent of the horror we were about to face.

from *Deja Dead* by Kathy Reichs

The following scene ending concludes a comic argument two senior women have about the best place to shop in New York City. The narrator is omniscient.

"Stop her, Phillip," Sally said, reaching for his hand. "Stop her or you'll find me in an early grave."

Alas, it was Edith who found one....

from *Control* by William Goldman

Character Endings

While the scene ending that focuses on plot reveals a change in the direction of the plot, the scene ending that focuses on character tends to reveal a change in the character or in our understanding of the character. This is referred to as an *insight*. This means that the reader knows the character better than she did before the scene ending. This character insight will probably be related to the development of a *theme*. Such endings can be presented in various ways.

THE I-KNOW-WHAT-THIS-MEANS INTERNAL MONOLOGUE

A character may reflect through internal monologue about the meaning of the events that occurred in that scene, for example, a mother and daughter argue about who will drive the car. The final lines of the scene could be the mother reflecting on how this is the beginning of many such arguments in which the daughter wants more independence. Or the scene might end from the daughter's point of view in which she concludes that her mother is a controlling maniac. Another variation might be one of the characters as an unreliable narrator (see "Nothing But the Truth" in chapter four) with the reader recognizing that the narrator is totally misreading the meaning of the argument. Perhaps the daughter isn't fighting for independence; rather, she is angry at her mother because she suspects her mom is having an adulterous affair. Or maybe the mother isn't being controlling. Instead, she is concerned that her daughter's recent uncharacteristic clumsiness might be an early sign of a debilitating disease that runs in the family, but the daughter knows nothing about it. In which case, driving might prove fatal.

Here are a couple of examples of this kind of scene ending. In both cases, notice how the narrator has some insight to share following an exchange of dialogue. In the first example, the character's thoughts are directly related to the conversation; in the second example, the insight is only set up by the dialogue, as a sort of framing device, but is not related to it.

"But haven't you ever wanted to work?"

"Oh, yes. Sometimes. It's just...I don't know. I never seem to get around to it."

And that was the long and short of it. He never seemed to get around to it. Every day for the last eighteen years he had got up in the morning with the intention of sorting out his career problem once and for all; as the day wore on, however, his burning desire to seek a place for himself in the outside world somehow got extinguished.

from *About a Boy* by Nick Hornby

She took a cab to the airport, Jerry the cabbie happy to see her. "Have fun in New York," he said, getting her bag out of the trunk. He liked her, or at least always acted as if he did. She called him 'Jare.'

"Thanks, Jare."

"You know, I'll tell you a secret: I've never been to New York. I'll tell you two secrets: I've never been on a plane." And he waved at her sadly as she pushed her way through the terminal door.

"Or an escalator!" he shouted.

The trick to flying safe, Zoë always said, was never to buy a discount ticket and to tell yourself you had nothing to live for anyway, so that when the plane crashed it was no big deal. Then when it didn't crash, when you had succeeded in keeping it aloft with your own worthlessness, all you had to do was stagger off, locate your luggage, and, by the time a cab arrived, come up with a persuasive reason to go on living.

from "You're Ugly, Too" by Lorrie Moore

POIGNANT DIALOGUE

A scene might end with dialogue. With this technique, a certain momentum is built up that suddenly stops at the end, like a runner smacking face-first into a lamppost. The effect is a little disorienting because the reader is caught up in the conversation, but it is also an opportunity to end at the height of a passionate or revealing exchange. The exact place where the dialogue ends can reveal a lot about the characters: what they're afraid of, what they hope for, how they are changing. The following example is from "You're Ugly, Too" by Lorrie Moore, excerpted above. This shows you how an author will vary the technique of scene endings. Here a depressed Zoë has come to visit her longtime girlfriend Evan, who complains about her boyfriend Charlie's many annoying habits, including watching football on a fuzzy screen because they don't have cable.

> Evan was beaming. "Oh, Zoë, I have something to tell you. Charlie and I are getting married."
> "Really." Zoë felt confused.
> "I didn't know how to tell you."
> "Yes, well, I guess the part about the fuzzy football misled me a little."
> "I was hoping you'd be my maid of honor," said Evan, waiting.
> "Aren't you happy for me?"
> "Yes," said Zoë, and she began to tell Evan a story about an award-winning violinist at Hilldale-Versailles, how the violinist had come home from competition in Europe and taken up with a local man, who made her go to all his summer softball games, made her cheer for him in the stands, with the wives, until later she killed herself. But when she got halfway through, to the part about cheering at the softball games, Zoë stopped.
> "What?" said Evan. "So what happened?"
> "Actually, nothing," said Zoë lightly. "She just really got into softball. I mean, really. You should have seen her."

Here we have a dialogue exchange ending the scene, but what makes the dialogue have so much impact is that Zoë doesn't say what she's thinking. Rather than warn her friend that she might lose her identity, she pulls back and lies to her. That notches up the conflict of the story by showing us Zoë doesn't approve of her friend's relationship. Now what will happen, we want to know?

A scene doesn't have to end with a stream of dialogue. Sometimes it may end with just one powerful line. In the following story, a father tells how he and his young daughter are coping after the death of his wife. This last paragraph of one of the scenes gets its emotional power from the offhand remark of the daughter.

> *My Jessica had to explain a neurologic disease she couldn't even pronounce. "I hate it when people ask me about Mom," she says. "I just tell them she fell off the Empire State Building."*
>
> from "Bridging" by Max Apple

POIGNANT DESCRIPTION

A scene can end with a description of the setting or a character doing something that seems mundane. The fact that the reader is focused on it is meant to elevate that simple setting or act to greater proportions. Say that we are writing about a teenage boy who is walking home after a silly fight with his girlfriend. He jumps out of the car, slams the door and marches down the lonely country road. Rather than focus on his thoughts, we might instead end the scene with a description of the moon: "The moon drifted among the dim clouds like a balloon escaped from a child's hand." The description isn't just there to describe the moon, but to establish that the metaphor is a reflection of the boy, too. Rather than stay and work out his relationship, he'd run off like a child, and unless he realizes it, his relationships may always escape his grasp and drift away from him.

The same effect can be achieved by focusing on a simple act. Let's use the same situation presented above: an angry teen walking home after a fight with his girlfriend. Instead of ending with a description of the untethered moon, the last lines can focus on a simple, inconsequential activity:

> *As he walked through the dark, Jimmy jumped up and snatched a leaf from a laurel tree hanging over the road. He*

placed it between his two thumbs just like his dad had taught him years ago and pushed his lips tight against his thumbs. He blew, hoping for the high-pitched squeal that had delighted him so much when his dad had done it. But the only sound he made now was the same one he'd made back then: a sloppy blubbering like a baby might make spitting out his creamed squash. All the way home Jimmy practiced, going through enough laurel leaves to clothe a whole tree. By the time he finally arrived home, he'd managed to produce a sound something like a cat being pitchforked. Nothing he'd show his dad.

This scene ending could show us that Jimmy is a stubborn boy, who, rather than reflect on what just happened with his girlfriend, prefers to distract himself with the leaves. Why the leaves? They might imply that Jimmy is just like his father, trying desperately to live up to his father's image. And if we know that his father is a twice-divorced minor league baseball player, we might infer that his dad is competitive and would rather win than compromise in his romantic relationships. A fate that seems to be waiting for Jimmy.

Notice how in these examples, the authors present only a description of the action, no commentary on it. The action is meant to convey a tone, a mood, as if we were staring at a painting.

He came out upon a ravine and ran along it until it began to draw away to the right and then plunged and slid down the embankment and leaped to clear the creek at the bottom. But the soft turf gave beneath his foot and he went face down in the water. When he tried to rise he could not. He got himself propped on his elbows, gasping, listening. The creek murmured away down the dark ravine. He leaned his face into the shallow water and drank, choking, and after a while he vomited. And after a while he drank again.

from *The Outer Dark* by Cormac McCarthy

He watches her as she walks toward the porch, silent and regal. There is the pad of feet, the clinking of dog tags as the dogs run for the house.

from "Territory" by David Leavitt

Final Word

I have written both genre and literary novels. I like both equally. I started as a writer of literary works: plays, short stories, poems (my first published book was a collection of poetry). Wanting to take a vacation from the emotional intensity of that kind of writing, I started a mystery. Once it was sold, I was hooked. Then, after writing a bunch of genre novels, I felt like exploring characters more deeply, so I returned to literary fiction. After writing four literary novels, I felt like I needed to get back to a more plot-driven story, so I wrote two genre novels. I don't think of one kind being more valuable than the other, nor is one kind easier to write than the other. The main difference is that I modify techniques to suit the kind of story I'm writing. Scene endings in my genre novels tend to be cliff-hangers, focusing on plot suspense (what will happen to the characters), while in my literary novels, they focus more on character suspense (how the characters feel about what is happening to them). The key words in that sentence are "tend" and "focus"; that means that most of the time that's the case. However, sometimes a genre novel needs to focus on character if the reader is to care about the plot, and a literary novel needs some good old-fashioned plot suspense if the reader is to care about characters.

Instant Workshop:
Endings That Don't

Look back at the Longfellow quote that started this chapter. He's referring to one of the most common maladies in writing endings: going on too long. When I was in graduate school studying poetry, I attended a writing workshop with another student, who was a first-rate poet. He had just one problem: Nearly every poem he wrote had an extra verse. This extra verse dragged the poem's momentum and dulled its effect. All he had to do was lop it off and the poem was instantly stronger. Poet Donald Hall, after fifteen drafts of "Ox Cart Man," decided to cut his final stanza. He was helped by the following advice from fellow poet Louis Simpson: "I'm pretty sure about omitting the last stanza—it's fidgety. And redundant." This is not an uncommon problem. When writers get to the end of anything—scene, chapter, stanza, poem—they get nervous that they haven't made their point. They quickly try to remedy the situation by adding a summary of what they've already done (thinking all along that they're being subtle). Here's a closing paragraph of a chapter from a student novel. Stephanie is at the bedside of her grown son, David, unconscious after a serious boating accident. Linda, David's wife, is still missing. Which lines, if any, need to be cut and why? (*Note:* The last line repeats a line Stephanie thought of earlier in the chapter. It's what she imagined her father would say to her if he were still alive.)

> *Stephanie felt as if she were loosing control of her life for the first time ever. She was a bit light-headed and weak-kneed, but managed to get back to the chair at David's bedside. Trembling hands covered her face. Her body shook uncontrollably in sobs that wouldn't stop. The realization that she could lose both David and Linda in one stupid boating incident was beginning to sink in, and all the Sutcliffe money and power in the world might not be enough to change that. Their destiny appeared to be completely out of Stephanie's hands. She wasn't used to that. She wasn't used to that at all. It was becoming too much for her to bear.*
> *"Don't cry, Steph, it just clouds the solution to the problem...."*

I would cut the last two sentences (from "It was becoming..." to the end) because they distract from the stronger line: "She wasn't used to that at all." The lines that follow stress her emotions, which the reader has already gotten enough of during that paragraph. Now the reader needs to know where that leaves Stephanie. Ending where I suggest tells us she's numbed to the point of inaction. That creates suspense about what she might do next—rally from the numbness or sink deeper into depression.

Try not to fall into this trap. Pay special attention to the final two or three paragraphs of each scene and hone them until they have an edge. This may mean rereading those endings again and again to get some objectivity about them. Donald Hall, referring to the stanza he eventually cut, said, "At the time, I thought it was the best thing in the poem! Watch out for what you think is best."

❈ 7 ❈

SHAPE TO FIT: FOCUSING A SCENE ON CHARACTER, PLOT OR THEME

"We may divide [fictional] characters into flat and round.... The test of a round character is whether it is capable of surprising us in a convincing way. If it never surprises, it is flat. If it does not convince, it is flat pretending to be round."

E.M. Forster

"When I am thickening my plots, I like to think 'What if...What if....'"

Patricia Highsmith

Remember those "reach out and touch someone" long-distance ads on television? Little kids talking gleefully with their tearful grandparents. Old friends calling each other as a weekly ritual, laughing over their childhood memories. A grown man calling his father for advice, and the moist-eyed dad proudly offering it. These ads brought tears to a nation's eyes for years. And there are plenty of ads that make you laugh every time you see them. But remember that no matter how clever, cute, funny or touching a commercial is, it is *selling* something.

So is a scene in a story.

Each scene is selling the reader one of the following products: character, plot or theme. As I've mentioned in previous chapters, the best scenes will offer some of each, yet only one of those products will be featured. A bookstore may offer a lot of different books, but the ones near the checkout counter are the ones it's featuring. A person may have a lot of different qualities, but the one she emphasizes is the one she wants you to notice, whether it's her wit, intelligence, face or body. That's what art does. It draws your attention to what the artist wants you to see, which is displayed in a certain way.

Depending upon what the writer wants the reader to take away from a scene, the writer uses different techniques to draw the reader's attention to what the writer wants him to see. The following is the same scene written from three different approaches, each emphasizing a focus on either character, plot or theme.

Focus on Character

This is an example of an opening scene that focuses on character. How can you tell? Read it first, then we'll discuss how it achieves this.

"Give me your hand. I'll tell you your fortune."

I sipped my coffee. "I was just hoping for a refill."

"Come on, Jake. What're you afraid of? Bad news?"

"Right now bad news would only improve my life."

Dedie wiped her hands on her apron and leaned over the counter. Her long curly red hair brushed the countertop. She snapped her fingers for me to give her my hand. "C'mon, you big baby, give it up."

"How come you don't wear a hair net?" I asked. "Isn't that against state law? Not to mention unsanitary."

She nodded toward Jimmy, the coffee shop owner, who sat at an empty booth reading USA Today. *He was a handsome man just starting to go fleshy. Ten years ago, he'd played the sexy neighbor on a midseason replacement sitcom that didn't get picked up for the fall. But he'd invested wisely and ended up owning a few coffee shops like this one.*

"Hear that music?" she said. Bob Dylan was singing "Idiot

Wind." He'd been mumble-singing since I'd come in about forty minutes ago.

"Doesn't sound like Jimmy's kind of music," I said.

"Hates Dylan. Neil Young is up next; hates him too. Tom Waits after that. Jimmy hates them all, says they all sound drunk. But he lets me play them. See those flowers." She gestured at the small white vases with a single fresh rose on each table. "My idea."

"Let me guess," I said. "He lets you have your way around here in exchange for telling his fortune."

"That's right. I predict which nights he's going to have sex with me."

I stuck out my hand. "What the hell then."

She laughed. I liked her laugh. It was a deep rumble, like a truck driving over gravel. She wasn't bad looking, her features too boyish to make her beautiful. I'd known her for almost a year now, as long as I'd been coming into Jimmy's. Jimmy I'd known since we were little kids and he'd kicked the crap out of me and stole my bicycle. I'd started a rumor at school that Jimmy had wanted to have sex with me and when I'd refused, he'd taken my bike. And that he'd threatened to beat me up every time he asked for sex and I refused. That got me my bike back and assured me Jimmy wouldn't beat on me again.

"Do you know what you're doing or is this bullshit?" I asked Dedie. "Not that I care. Just curious."

"I been taking lessons from a real psychic. She said I had natural ability, that I just needed to train it some." She pressed her fingers into my palm. It felt kind of sexy.

I shouted over to the booth, "Hey, Jimmy, I'm stealing your girl."

He waved his hand without looking up from the newspaper.

"Fine. As long as she doesn't give you free refills."

"Princes don't come any more charming than that," I joked, turning back to Dedie. "So, what do you see? Something involving cashflow, I hope."

"Let's take a look," she said, spreading my fingers out like dead starfish. She frowned and quickly laid my hand down on the counter.

"What?" I said, vaguely disturbed, even though I didn't believe in any of that hocus-pocus.
"Nothing," she said. "Guess I need more training." She
turned and hurried away, her rubber soles squeaking like
scared mice.

Now, let's look at the factors that help focus this scene on
character:

1. Characterization. What does the reader come away with
from this scene? Does the reader have any idea what the
story is about? No. What the writer is selling here is characterization with a couple side orders of tone and foreshadowing. He hopes that the reader will like the
characters—especially Jake—enough to want to continue
along with him on his day. He wants the reader to snack
on tone: to find Jake amusing, the kind of good-natured
fellow who's always good company. Toward that end he
lets the reader know that Jake's fallen on hard times
("Right now bad news would only improve my life"), but
he maintains a sense of humor about it. This immediately makes him sympathetic.

2. Foreshadowing. Because the author is fresh out of any plot
conflict that indicates what this story is going to be about,
he instead offers the reader a rain check in the form of
ominous foreshadowing. The fact that Dedie drops his
hand and runs off tells the reader there's probably trouble
ahead (reinforced by the simile "her rubber soles squeaking like scared mice").

Focusing on character means being aware of what the
character wants and introducing that as soon as possible.
There are two kinds of character "wants." The ultimate want,
which is what the story is about but the protagonist may or
may not realize it, and the immediate want, which is often
symbolic of the ultimate want and is what he wants right now
in this scene. Kurt Vonnegut put it this way: "When I used to
teach creative writing, I would tell the students to make characters want something right away—even if it's only a glass of
water. Characters paralyzed by the meaningless of modern life

still have to drink water from time to time."

Focus on Plot
Now let's take the same scene setup that has been rewritten to focus on plot.

> *"Give me your hand. I'll tell you your fortune."*
>
> *I sipped my coffee, keeping one eye on the front door. "I'd settle for a refill."*
>
> *"Come on, Jake. What're you afraid of?"*
>
> *What was I afraid of? Where to start? That she'd see my hand shaking like a junkie on the third day in detox. That she'd feel the cold sweat slicking my palms, puddling between my fingers. That any minute a couple guys pretending to be with the FBI would come busting through the front door, wave a phony warrant and whisk me off this wobbly stool, never to be heard from again. That the envelope in my left pocket would never get to the woman I'd been paid to deliver it to. Which meant a whole lot of innocent people were going to die tonight.*
>
> *I wiped my hands on my pants, felt my elbow brush my gun clipped to my belt under my sports jacket. Extra clips weighed down both pockets in my jacket. They bulged as if I'd just won the nickel slots in Vegas.*
>
> *"Is it me you don't trust, Jake, or women in general?"*
>
> *"Women in specific," I said. "Waitresses in general."*
>
> *She grinned, poured some fresh coffee into my cup. "Hey, Jimmy, I think your pal just insulted me."*
>
> *Jimmy, the coffee shop owner, sat at an empty booth reading USA Today. He was a handsome man just starting to go fleshy. Ten years ago he'd played the sexy neighbor on a mid-season replacement sitcom that didn't get picked up for the fall. But he'd invested wisely and ended up owning a few coffee shops like this one. I was here to see him but hadn't quite worked up the nerve to tell him why. He was normally pretty low-key, but this would rattle him. I might have to club him a few times with my gun, which I hated to do to a friend.*
>
> *"He insults everybody," Jimmy said, without looking up, "just by being in the same room with them." He snickered and turned the page.*

> On the other hand, a solid clubbing might do him some good.
>
> The door opened and I spun around, my hand diving into my jacket, clamping onto my gun. I had it half out of the holster before I saw it was just a young couple with a baby. The father, in his early twenties, grabbed a high chair and carried it to a table in the back. Presumably not to annoy other customers when the baby started to cry. That was good. If there was shooting, there was less chance they'd be hit back there.
>
> "C'mon, Jake," Dedie said. "I need the practice."
>
> "Do you know what you're doing or is this bullshit?" I asked her.
>
> "I been taking lessons from a real psychic. She said I had natural ability, that I just needed to train it some." She reached for my right hand. I pulled it back and dropped it into my lap, closer to the gun. I reached out my left hand. "I'm used to doing the right hand," she said.
>
> I didn't say anything, I just let the left hand lay there on the counter top.
>
> "Fine," she said, pouting. "The left hand is the devil's hand, Jake. Did you know that?"
>
> "What do you see? Fame and fortune? A long trip? A beautiful woman? If you take requests, I'd prefer the long trip."
>
> She spread my fingers out like dead starfish. She pressed her fingers into my palm. At first it hurt, as if she were trying to rub off something she didn't like. She frowned and quickly laid my hand down on the counter.
>
> "What?" I said, vaguely disturbed, even though I didn't believe in any of that hocus-pocus.
>
> "Nothing," she said. "Guess I just can't do the left hand yet." She turned and hurried away, banging her hip on the counter as she bolted.

Here's how this scene focuses on plot:

1. Right from the beginning, the reader's attention is being focused on the plot: "I sipped my coffee, keeping one eye on the front door." That tells the reader that at any moment someone may come through the door.
2. Where the character focus scene let the characters banter

for a few lines, the plot focus scene jumps into Jake's internal monologue to set the stakes: "What am I afraid of?" This line is followed by a list that tells the reader what is going on and that many lives hang in the balance.

3. Where character focus emphasized Jake's wit and charm, the plot focus emphasizes his fear. Whomever he's up against, they are formidable. They have the ability to produce fake FBI IDs and warrants, so Jake can't look to anybody around him for help.

4. Instead of Jimmy just being an old boyhood friend characterized by an amusing story, the childhood story is omitted which, because of the light tone, would have reduced the suspense. Instead, it is revealed that Jake needs Jimmy's help and is not above clubbing Jimmy to get it.

5. We know Jake is a much harder man than the character focus Jake. Here he watches the family and is relieved they will be safer, but he doesn't leave or hurry to Jimmy to insure their safety. Plus, he only gives the waitress his left hand in order to keep his right hand free to draw his gun.

6. Dedie bumping her hip is more serious than her shoes squeaking like mice. There are lots of other small details designed to add to the ominousness, but those are the main points.

Focus on Theme

There are many different ways to focus on theme. I could strip away most description and let it come out through the nuances in the dialogue. Or I could strip away much of the dialogue and let it come out through the de-

TIP

Stir Plot Till Thickens

One problem writers have with plot is that they play it too safe. They write along the conventional, familiar plotlines they've seen so often themselves. I encourage my students to do what I do: "Write yourself into a corner." Yup, it's just like painting yourself in a corner. You placed your characters in a position so that even you don't know what they'll do next. This doesn't necessarily mean it has to be a contrived cliff-hanger. It could place them in a tricky moral dilemma in which both choices are unacceptable—at the time. Not only does this make the story more interesting, but it forces the writer to think with greater depth about the plot and what the plot means to the characters involved. It's what F. Scott Fitzgerald meant when he said, "All good writing is swimming under water and holding your breath."

scription and action. There is no right or best way. It depends on the writer's style and skill.

> *"Give me your hand. I'll tell you your fortune."*
>
> *I sipped my coffee, my third cup. I was already twenty minutes late. "Sure, why not?"*
>
> *"Really?" she said, delighted. "You'd be surprised how many people get spooked. Black arts, witchcraft and all that."*
>
> *"I don't believe in anything, so you're safe with me."*
>
> *Dedie gave me a funny look, the expression of a woman on a blind date who's just found out her escort is out of work. "I never know when you're kidding, Jake."*
>
> *"Me neither." I laid my hand on the counter, stretching the fingers out until the skin in my palm felt taut and the cross-hatched lines of my future nearly disappeared.*
>
> *Dedie wiped her hands on her apron and leaned over the counter. Her straight red hair looked as if it had been hacked off in a fit of anger, giving her a Joan of Arc look. She was my age but had the look of someone who would read my list of complaints about life and toss it back in my face with a contemptuous snort. Secretly, I wanted her to.*
>
> *She took my hand in hers, gently laying it on top of hers. My hand relaxed, the fingers cupping slightly like the curdled legs of a dead spider. With her free hand she slipped her glasses out of her apron and put them on. She leaned closer to my hand. Her mouth opened slightly and I noticed a chip of red lipstick on her top front tooth. Somehow that gave her even more credence.*
>
> *"Hey, Jimmy," she said, "he's got the same fortune line as you."*
>
> *She nodded toward Jimmy the coffee shop owner who sat at an empty booth reading USA Today. He was a handsome man just starting to go fleshy. Ten years ago he'd played the sexy neighbor on a midseason replacement sitcom that didn't get picked up for the fall. But he'd invested wisely and ended up owning a few coffee shops like this one.*
>
> *"Zat so?" Jimmy said, nodding. "Then you're in for a secure future, Jake."*
>
> *I looked at my watch. Thirty minutes late. Secure future,*

huh. I wasn't worried about future security. Hell, that's exactly what I was trying to get away from.

Dedie's fingers plowed roughly along the lines of my palm. She was muttering something to herself.

"What?" I asked. "I can't hear you."

She looked up at me startled, her skin reddening as if I'd just busted in on her in the shower. "Nothing. Sometimes I think aloud. Dumb habit. Forget it."

I tried to but it was still disconcerting. I checked my watch again. No way was I stepping out of this place until I was a solid hour late.

"I see you wear a cross," I said to Dedie. "You Catholic?"

"I don't know. I was raised Catholic. I kinda drifted. You know."

"But you believe in God?"

"Yeah, some kind of God. I'm not sure what kind, though."

"The kind who would give us free will? Let us make our own mistakes?"

"What're you getting at, Jake?" She dropped my hand on the counter, anger building because she knew by my tone that I was laying a trap.

"Well, what kind of God would stick your future on your hand like a price bar? Kind of screws with that whole free will, have faith thing."

Her fingers lifted to touch her dangling gold cross. She seemed surprised to find it still there, as if she thought I might have stolen it somehow. "What's wrong with you, Jake? You used to be such a sweet guy."

I held up my hand and pushed it toward her face. "Can't you tell?"

She opened her mouth as if to tell me exactly what was wrong with me. Instead she closed her mouth, shook her head and walked away. "You'd better hurry, Jake. If you're more than an hour late, they might actually do something about it. Then where would you be?"

Here's how this scene emphasizes theme:

1. The differences from the first two versions are clear right from the opening. Instead of teasing about having his hand

read or being nervous about who might come through the door, Jake is distracted by being late for work: "I sipped my coffee, my third cup. I was already twenty minutes late. 'Sure, why not?'" From this the reader realizes that the real conflict for Jake is not going to take place here in this coffee shop. Instead, the reader is shown that even though Jake is twenty minutes late, he decides to stay for this frivolous (to him) activity. He has some problem at work, but the reader doesn't know what it is. What makes this a focus of theme and not plot is that the stakes are more personal, less dramatic. No one's coming through the door with guns. Jake's problems are internal, as the reader learns throughout this scene, and related to his attitude.

2. The Jake in this scene is not as charming as the one in the other versions; his humor is more cutting, meaner. The section in which he announces that he doesn't "believe in anything" reveals him to be cynical, though the reader hasn't yet determined if that's true or if he's just an unreliable narrator. Also, Dedie's response to him is more serious. The simile about her expression is one of shock and her dialogue ("I never know when you're kidding, Jake") tells the reader she takes him seriously. The Dedie of the first two versions would not have taken him seriously, but because we're focusing on theme, the reader can only take Jake seriously if someone else does. Otherwise, the reader may just think of him as being a churlish whiner.

3. Most of the similes have changed. Similes need to match the tone of the focus. The first two versions had more comical similes; this version implies more depth. When Jake says, "I laid my hand on the counter, stretching the fingers out until the skin in my palm felt taut and the crosshatched lines of my future nearly disappeared," he's using subtle imagery that suggests he thinks he has no future. That's at the core of what's bothering him and somehow his job is related to that. Later, when Dedie takes his hand, he describes it in the same dead way: "My hand relaxed, the fingers cupping slightly like the curdled legs of a dead spider."

4. The description of Dedie has changed. Instead of the long,

curly red hair, which is more sensual, her hair is awk-
wardly cut to remind Jake of Joan of Arc, someone who
was able to make a leap of faith and do something active.
The opposite of him, who sits there so he can be late, a
cowardly, passive-aggressive move.

5. Jimmy, the owner, has changed too. Where before he was
just a lump at a booth, now he's friendly and encouraging
to both Dedie and Jake. This provides another contrast to
Jake's gloom. Jimmy's background story of failure as an
actor but bouncing back as the owner of several restaurants contrasts Jake's childish attitude. In fact, the reader
discovers that Jake's conflict has to do with wanting to get
away from the "secure future," like Benjamin in *The Graduate*.

6. Where the other two versions focused on the palm reading
as an ominous foreshadowing, here it is merely the catalyst for Jake to launch into a diatribe about free will, which
is the central theme that the story's conflict seems to be reflecting. But, ironically, Dedie's last few lines ("You'd better
hurry, Jake. If you're more than an hour late, they might actually do something about it. Then where would you be?")
are real insight that is the result of Jake's behavior, not the
lines on his palm.

Final Words

These three versions are not the only way to achieve the focus
that you want. They are only examples of one way. There are a
multitude of different approaches, some more subtle, others
more aggressive. The trick is to find your voice, your own
unique approach. And, as with the other techniques we've covered, no scene has to be either one thing or another; it can be
a combination. If I were to actually start a novel with the sam-
ple scene used above, my final version would be completely different than, yet have elements of, all of them.

TIP

A Closer Look at Theme

A full examination of theme is for another place. Many of my students balk when I discuss theme and show how writers subtly weave it throughout their works. "Are they really thinking all that when they write?" they ask, suddenly frightened that they have no idea what their "theme" is. Theme is the reason the events we're reading about are happening; they reveal the universal in all of our actions. However, not all books, even well-written books, develop a deliberate theme. Some books just want to tell a compelling story. Again, you should write the kind of book you want to read, but a good writer shouldn't limit her horizons. Herman Melville was a best-selling writer of adventure stories before he befriended the more literary writer, Nathaniel Hawthorne. As a result of their friendship, Melville developed an interest in more literary writing. The result was Moby Dick, *a novel that ruined his career (hardly sold at all) but cemented his literary reputation for hundreds of years to come. However, if dwelling on theme is not for you, don't sell other writers short. The best writers use theme to structure the plot of the story. Here are a few writers discussing their themes.*

Bret Easton Ellis, discussing his novel Glamorama, *explained that the theme he had in mind was the tyranny of beauty: "The insecurity the beauty machine foists upon us is not so different than the insecurity that terrorists are aiming for. They blow up government offices, but really their main objective is to make us feel insecure [in our daily routine]. It's to make us feel unsafe in our lives and to get so sick of it that we give in to their demands. It's about fear. The metaphorical leap I was making in* Glamorama *was connecting the two."*

*For novelist William Boyd (*A Good Man in Africa*), a consistent theme is that "my heroes...usually...[recognize] that the universe is utterly indifferent to the fate of individuals."*

*Scott Spencer (*Endless Love*), focuses on "someone's path to knowledge being a kind of madness. I'm interested in the route that people must take to arrive at a spot where they can be large and whole and responsive. And the kind of forbearance that we need to show each other because sometimes people can be doing things that seem really crazy and nonsensical, but when you look back at it, this was the path that they had to take, there was no other way to get there."*

Instant Workshop:
Creating Characters with Character

W. Somerset Maugham once said, "You can never know enough about your characters." However, when you *first* start writing about characters, you don't have to know too much about them. You just write and try to capture their voices. But once you've sketched a character into your story, you need to develop who that person is. Many writers use a character chart, such as the one I use, which is shown on the next page. Filling in these details gives me a chance to think about my characters with more depth. The trick is to not rush through this chart, filling anything in just to get it done. Rather, think about each entry and what effect that has on the character, for example, we know how much appearance affects how people are treated and how they view themselves, either positively or negatively. What if that stereotypically svelte woman was a few pounds heavier? How would that affect who she is, how she sees herself, how others see her, how she acts? And so on with each category. Especially important is deciding what the character wants, which will determine plot and how that character interacts with the other characters. (*Note*: If you have room, pin these sheets to your bulletin board or place them in a notebook for easy reference when you need to remember a character's hair color or the kind of car he drives. I refer to these sheets constantly, which saves a lot of time thumbing through early chapters for the information.)

Character Development Worksheet

Name:

What does he/she want?

What will he/she get?

What gets in the way of what he/she wants?

Physical description

age: height: weight:

eyes: hair: build:

health: voice:

scars, marks:

clothing:

Living situation

occupation:

car: home:

pets:

Personal characteristics

goals:

attitude:

habits/mannerisms:

peeves: sports:

hobbies: magazines/books:

movies: music:

motives:

Background

birthplace:

parents: spouse/lover:

children:

military: education:

☙ 8 ☙.

THE P³ EQUATION:
MAKING PAYOFF
SCENES WORK

> *"A great writer creates a world of his own and his
> readers are proud to live in it. A lesser writer
> may entice them for a moment, but soon he will
> watch them filing out."*
>
> Cyril Connolly

You've spent a long, hot day mowing the lawn, or cooking a tasty and nutritional family dinner or struggling through the shark-infested waters of your job. Why bother? What's the payoff? Neighborhood pride, family obligations, money, work ethic? Those are all good reasons, but none are as satisfying as having a loved one come up to you after your exhausting labors, give you a hug and say, "Boy, the lawn looks great." Or, "This meal is delicious. Can I have more?" Or, "Thanks for working those extra hours so we could go on vacation." The first list of payoffs has the satisfaction level of checking an item off a long to do list. The second list of payoffs, however, gives a feeling of accomplishment beyond the deed itself, as if what you have done has an impact beyond the event. The payoffs of your scenes must also have an impact beyond the event itself. The *payoff* is fulfilling the promise that the scene makes to the reader.

Wanna See Something Really Cool?

Each scene makes a *promise* to the reader. An action scene promises that by the end of the scene, the reader will be breathless with excitement and either relieved that the characters pulled through the adventure or sad that they didn't. A love scene promises that there will be an attempt to bring the couple together for physical contact and, though this attempt may succeed or fail, when it is over, the reader will feel satisfied with the outcome. And so on.

The promise is nothing more than a variation of one kid carrying a shoe box, walking up to another kid and saying, "Wanna see something really cool?" Who can resist the thrilling anticipation as the kid with the box slowly, so slowly, lifts the edge of the lid, revealing nothing but a sliver of darkness. But wait! The overhead light in the boy's room begins to eat away the darkness in the box and you can see something. A shape is forming. My God, it's a...

Whatever.

In the promise part of the scene, it doesn't matter what's in the box. The promise has only one function: to tease the reader into being compelled to see how the scene turns out. In other words, to get the reader as interested as possible in looking in that box. In the payoff part of the scene, the reader discovers what's in the box and how it affects the two boys.

The main method of increasing the promise value is by increasing the *stakes*. I have a simple way of teaching my students about stakes. I walk into the room the first day of class, take out a quarter and flip it into the air. I ask a student to call it, heads or tails. I then show them the results. Everyone looks curious ("What is he up to?"), but a bit bored ("So what?"). Then I offer a challenge: "I'll flip the coin again. This time, if you win, you get an automatic A in the class, you never have to show up or write any assignments. But..." (a dramatic pause to increase suspense) "if you lose, you get an automatic F, plus you must show up every day of class and do all the assignments, even though you will get an F. Any takers?" Now I have their full interest. A couple clowns always raise their hands to accept the challenge, but I give them the steely stare and say, "I'm serious. If you lose, you will get an F on your transcripts." They usually back down. One person always accepts the bet and I flip the coin high into the air. Every student watches the coin arcing up and dropping down. I slap it onto my wrist, peek, grin and say to the student, "Are you sure? Are you positive you want this bet?" They always hesitate. Others advise them, "Don't do it, man!" or "Go for it!" Of course, I welch on the bet: If they lose, I don't fail them (though I don't tell them that until the end of class, so the lesson of stakes sticks with them); if they win, I pocket the coin without showing them because I've already made my point. The higher the stakes, the greater the intensity of the promise and, of course, the bigger the payoff must be. This is what I call the P^3 Equation: "Payoffs Per Promise." The greater the promise section of a scene is, the greater the payoff should be.

The two principal ways to increase the stakes are through *character* and *plot*. By enhancing either or both of these elements, the stakes go up and so does the promise.

Now, let's take the same little boy-with-a-shoe-box scenario and crank up the stakes. As it stands, the kid with the box just wants to show it to the other kid. Simple transaction. But what if we add a little information?

> *Bill leaned over the water fountain and let the cool water wash over his sore lip. Who'd have thought his baby sister would have such a grip? She was only ten months old and face grabbing was her newest trick. The constellation of scabs on his cheeks proved that much. Still, it was almost worth it to see her laugh so much when she got a chubby fistful of his face.*
>
> *"Wanna see something cool?" the voice behind him asked.*
>
> *Bill straightened up, wiped his mouth. "I don't want to see your smelly old sneakers." He reached for the box.*
>
> *"Careful!" Carl said, pulling the box out of Bill's reach. "This ain't sneakers, my friend. Not by a long shot."*

The difference here is that Bill is developed a little more as a character. The sentences describing his baby sister are there to create sympathy for Bill: He's the kind of kid who loves his ten-month-old sister. Because we like that about Bill, we don't want anything bad to happen to him. The stakes of opening that box have gone up.

Another way to go is to develop Carl's character, but not sympathetically:

> *Bill watched Carl coming down the hall carrying a beat-up old shoe box in front of him as if it was filled with crystal and*

might break at the slightest bump. Not that there was any chance of a bump from any of the other students in the hall; they all kept their distance as usual. Nobody wanted to risk getting Carl mad. Not after what he'd done to Jimmy Pine last week. In fact, Bill was surprised to see Carl at school. Wasn't he still on suspension?

Bill hurriedly grabbed his books out of his locker so he could escape before Carl got to him. For some unknown reason, Carl thought Bill was his friend. He yanked on his notebook, but it was wedged between his chemistry and history books. Come on! He yanked again, harder.

"Hey, Bill, wanna see something cool?" Carl said behind him.

Too late. And what was that smell?

In this version, the concentration is on making Carl's character as sinister as possible. The fact that Carl was suspended tells us he's done something bad and may do something worse. The fact that he's in school when he's still on suspension suggests that whatever is in that box may be directed at the school. The stakes are greater now because the possibility of what is in the box may affect more than just these two boys.

Both of the above versions concentrate on character, but there are also plot elements present. You can focus more on one element than the other, but you can't do one at the exclusion of the other. One of the techniques used when focusing on plot is *foreshadowing*, which is a kind of promise. There are different forms of foreshadowing. One form is a character trait. In the opening of *Marathon Man*, Babe's dogged competitiveness against another runner who is better than he is demonstrates that Babe has an inner strength he can tap into. Another form is a physical item. In the beginning of *Moby Dick*, the inn's dark painting is of the whalers being overwhelmed by a whale. Playwright Anton Chekhov said that if there's a gun hanging on the wall in the first act, by the third act that gun must be fired. What he meant was, the gun is an implied promise for which there must be a payoff.

Let's look at the same shoe box scene written with a focus

on plot:

> *Carl felt the sweat drops etching down his forehead straight for*
> *his eyes. He let them. He couldn't risk taking even one hand*
> *from the shoe box. He shuffled down the hallway, afraid to lift*
> *his feet for fear he might trip. He was a star track and field ath-*
> *lete who hadn't tripped since he was five. But today was not the*
> *day to take that chance. Not with what he was carrying.*
>
> *"Hey, Carl, whatchya got there? Your smelly sneakers?" Bill*
> *appeared at his side, bouncing happily along. He reached for*
> *the box.*
>
> *"No!" Carl snapped, spinning away.*
>
> *"Jesus, man, take a pill. What the hell is that?"*

Where the previous versions directed the reader's attention at the characters first and the box second, here almost every line is about the box. The author is pointing at it and saying to the reader, "Whatever you do, don't take your eye off the box." Plot focus is on what will happen, whereas character focus is on who it will happen to.

What You Write Is What They Get

Just as in life, making a promise is easy. Keeping it is the hard part, which is why the payoff part of the scene is where writers most often fail. Remember, each scene is like a complete story in itself. How many stories have you read in which the beginning was exciting and full of promise, only to have a disappointing ending that never delivered on the promise? No one can tell you how to write a satisfying payoff; however, you can be taught what elements to look for and what pitfalls to avoid.

As with the promise, the payoff will either concentrate on plot or character. Plot payoffs will startle the reader with a shift in plot: something will happen to the characters or they will do something that will alter their *external* circumstances. Character payoffs will startle the reader with a shift in character: the characters will be *internally* affected or changed by what has happened.

The key to a good payoff, plot or character, is not that you give the reader what you think she wants. The hero does not have to succeed in each action scene; the lovers do not have to embrace in each love scene. When you try to do that, you often end up writing a predictable scene that only disappoints. Recently in my script workshop, a student turned in a script he was writing about World War II. The first Nazi he described had "an acne-scarred face." "Why?" I asked him. "Because he's a Nazi and I want him to look ugly." However, because they've seen this acne-scarred Nazi a million times before, the audience will register the familiar image and the level of promise is immediately reduced. The audience knows that if they have a cliché like this in the promise, how original can the payoff be? Indeed, the payoff of this student's scene was a car chase in which the Nazis end up crashing their car and it explodes. Since they've also seen this conclusion to a car chase a million times, the audience will stop having faith that anything good will happen in this story.

The same problem can occur in character-driven payoffs. A student in my novel workshop submitted a chapter in which the two main characters, who were on the verge of falling in love, coincidentally found themselves on the same flight home. They wanted to sit together, so the man, Bill, asked the ticket holder beside the woman, Susan, to swap seats. He said sure and left. Now, there's nothing wrong with that. In fact, it's realistic in that most people would probably be accommodating. However, because this was the first extended scene of the couple together, the tension (promise) would have been heightened if the man was not so accommodating. If Bill and/or Susan had been forced to somehow convince the man to move, either by bribery, cajoling, lying or some other interesting means, the plot would have been more interesting and their characters would have been richer. Instead of just talking and thinking about their relationship, this would have been an overt act that demonstrated not only how much they wanted to be together (the stakes), but the kind of people they were by how they went about achieving it. Were they clever, bullying, blunt, clumsy? Plus, there was an opportunity to see either their contrasting styles in approaching this problem or their ability to work well together, picking up on each other's cues.

There is nothing intrinsically wrong with the way she wrote it—they asked for the seat, the man obliged—except that the rest of the chapter consisted of Bill and Susan talking about their troubles, flirting a little, then getting off the plane and driving into town together. But the dialogue was mostly information about what they'd been doing and how hard it had been on them. Without the small complication of having to do something specific to secure the seats next to each other, the scene seemed too contrived to get them into their seats so they could start yakking. By throwing a roadblock at them, she would have made the scene more compelling for the reader to find out what would happen.

The payoff in this case is the conversation. For the payoff conversation to satisfy, it must do several things: (1) It must reveal more of the characters than the reader has seen before, both informationally and emotionally. Information is provided about the characters that the reader and/or other character didn't know about. This could be background from their past or something concerning the current plotline. Emotionally, the characters' reactions to each other are different than they have been before, being somehow intensified by the information they have received or the situation they are in. The reader must feel as though she knows these characters feelings much more deeply because of this scene. (2) The dialogue must be fresh and unlike anything the reader has read before. This will be achieved by making sure each speaker's voice is distinct and reflects his or her personality. Every person has a unique rhythm to the way they speak, just as they have a unique walk. Beginning writers often have their characters speak in the same voice and cadence, making their dialogue basically interchangeable. (3) The final payoff is watching the impact of what has just happened on the characters. When the winner is announced at the Academy Awards, the camera immediately cuts to reaction shots of the losers. Or on *Sally Jesse Raphael*, when Girl X confesses to Girl Z, her "best friend," that she's been sleeping with Girl Z's husband, the camera is focused on Girl Z to capture the impact of that information. In your scene, the impact can be visible or not. External or internal. It doesn't matter. What matters is that the reader feels that whatever the impact the scene had on the characters is enough of a payoff to justify the existence of that scene.

Final Word

So far I've described how promise and payoff work within a scene. However, stories, novels and movies have specific scenes that are designated as payoff scenes. They are the tent poles around which the rest of the story is built. Action scenes, sex scenes and comic scenes are the payoff for the previous promise scenes. In heist stories such as *Entrapment, Mission: Impossible* and *Thief,* one obvious payoff scene is when they break into the impregnable location and steal the invaluable gizmo. What the audience wants to see in such a scene is cleverness from the thief in overcoming the safeguards (cool gadgets), some physical daring (hanging from the ceiling) and something unexpectedly going wrong, resulting in an improvised clever escape.

Some writers balk at the thought that there are formulas to writing, but all we're listing are the ingredients. A Caesar salad contains such and such. However, two different people cooking the same recipe will not produce the same dish. The one who is more creative and innovative will concoct something that transcends formula. The writer needs to be especially inventive and clever in conjuring payoffs. A weak payoff scene is where readers, especially editors, stop reading because there is no reason to believe the rest of the book will get any better.

In the following chapters, we will explore how to get the most out of the various types of payoff scenes.

❊ 9 ❊.
Hello, Stranger:
First Meetings

"Advice to young writers who want to get ahead without any annoying delays: don't write about Man, write about a man."

E.B. White

Can you remember the first time you met the person you eventually fell in love with? Probably. It was a life-altering moment, even if you didn't know it at the time. Sometimes people recognize such moments as they are happening, sometimes they don't. The same is true for characters in a story. However, the big difference between fiction and real life is that in fiction, such momentous meetings aren't for the benefit of the participants, but for the benefit of the reader. A "first meeting" scene is designed to affect the reader in some way that contributes to his understanding of and involvement in the story.

How the reader is affected is determined by the author adjusting a single control knob: information given to the reader. This type of information is referred to as *superior knowledge* because the reader is aware of more than the characters in the scene. How much and what kind of superior knowledge the author gives prior to the meeting determines how the reader will react during both the promise and payoff portions of the meeting scene. The reader, for example, may already know that the two characters will eventually become lovers. He knows this because the meeting is told in flashback, or there is dialogue about two characters he already knows have been married for thirty years. Or it might be a historical novel and this is the first meeting of Cleopatra and Julius Caesar or Samson and Delilah. The reader's attitude toward such a meeting is very different than if he was reading about two characters he knew nothing about.

The first step is for the writer to decide what effect she hopes the scene will have on the reader; the second step is to use the superior knowledge tool to achieve it. The knowledge can be imparted to the reader during the promise, payoff or both. How much is given, in what combination and where all contribute to altering the effect on the reader. It's like adding liquid to a glass and then hitting the glass with a spoon. Adjusting the level of liquid changes the tone when the glass is struck.

There are many different kinds of first meetings, and the reader expects such a scene to be special. It doesn't have to be elaborate, wacky or melodramatic, though it could be. It just means that the reader must feel a heightened sense that this scene is important, and when finishing it, he must feel satisfied. Some examples of significant first meetings:

- protagonist and antagonist. This is the main character of the story and the person who stands in his way of getting what he wants, or the "hero" and the "villain." However, the so-called villain can turn out to be a good person, but the protagonist doesn't recognize it yet.
- ex-lovers or ex-spouses who haven't seen each other in years after an acrimonious split-up.
- child and parent who haven't seen each other in years after an acrimonious split-up.
- soon-to-be-lovers Type A: one is good and the other is obviously not good, though the good one can't see it.
- soon-to-be-lovers Type B: they're both good and obviously made for each other, but they don't get along at first.
- protagonist and an archetypal figure: for example, a Charon/ferryman character who takes the character from a familiar world to an unfamiliar one, such as the cabdriver in the Scorsese film *After Hours* or the gondolier in Thomas Mann's *Death in Venice*.

This is not a definitive list. There are many variations and additions. Mystery novels are mostly first meetings: The detective keeps interviewing suspects and people with information crucial to the case. Each of those meetings must somehow be special or the whole novel seems repetitious and mundane. In science fiction, first meetings with aliens also demand a special touch, especially since the target audience has seen dozens of such encounters before. Romance novels by their covers promise a dynamic first meeting between the lovers. From genre to mainstream, each has its own kind of first meetings, but each demands the same result—something memorable.

First Meetings: The Promise

In essence, the promise portion is about *anticipation*—getting the reader excited about what's to come. As previously mentioned, the level of anticipation is directly related to the amount and kind of information you give the reader. It's as if you wanted to take your kids to Walt Disney World. Would you tell them first so they could enjoy the anticipation of going, or would you tell them the family's going to visit Uncle Zeke with the hairy nostrils and instead pull up to the Magic Kingdom and shout, "Surprise"? Both approaches to storytelling are legitimate and effective. If you choose to build the anticipation, the promise portion will be longer and more involved. If you choose surprise, skip to the "First Meetings: The Payoff" section.

Earlier we discussed Stanley Elkin's story "A Poetics for Bullies," in which Push the Bully dominates his circle of adolescent acquaintances until one day a new kid shows up (page 104). Elkin could have Push just run into the new kid, but instead he created suspense about this boy by having someone talk about him first. The miniscene continues with Push tormenting Eugene while Eugene tries to tell him about the new kid. As Push forces water on him, Eugene manages to utter a few more "promises" to the reader about the kid: "He's got this funny accent—you could die." "He has this crazy haircut." The construction of this scene has two main purposes:

1. To create suspense about Push meeting the new kid—a collision of two powerful forces.
2. To show Push as being more interested in dominating Eugene than in hearing Eugene's news. By the end of the scene, when Push says, "Well then, let's go see this new kid of yours," the reader's anticipation has been heightened because of the information he's been given. (The payoff of this scene is discussed later in "First Meetings: The Payoff.")

A similar promise technique is used in the James Stewart Western, *Destry Rides Again* (later remade with Audie Murphy). In this case, the town drunk tells the villain who runs the town that he's sent for the son of famous lawman Tom Destry to clean up the town. He delivers a lengthy speech about all the rough and tough things that Tom Destry did before he died. It is indeed an impressive resume. Cut to the stagecoach arriving, the one with Tom Destry's son in it. Half the town is standing at the station waiting to meet this Destry fellow. The stagecoach door opens and a large burly man with big guns strapped to his side jumps out, yanks the driver down and punches him for such a bumpy ride. The villain and his henchmen look stunned and afraid while the town titters with hope. The old-timer cackles I-told-you-so, runs over to the hulk and starts pumping his hand, welcoming the son of the legendary lawman. "I'm not Destry," the man says, annoyed. "I'm Destry," comes a voice from someone still in the coach. He steps out holding a birdcage and a frilly parasol. The bystanders burst out laughing. The villains heckle. He smiles good-naturedly and helps a woman out of the stage (the items are hers). One of the villains makes a threatening move toward him, hand on gun. Destry points out that he's not wearing guns, doesn't believe in them. The townspeople look disappointed, the villains look delighted. They slap him on the back and lead him to the saloon for a drink. Of course, the movie's payoff is already implied: Eventually Destry will strap on his guns (he is his father's boy after all) and clean up the town. But this first meeting scene uses the promise of the town drunk: A really tough lawman is coming. Then it uses that expectation to deliver a payoff to the scene that surprises the audience: He's not a tough guy after all. The underlying suspense is established: How will this nonviolent, nontough guy clean up a town of violent tough guys?

Another variation of the first meeting scene is the *serial* first meeting. Basically, this is a series of first meeting scenes strung together in order to introduce the main characters. The classic example is *The Magnificent Seven* (or the Japanese film it was based on, *The Seven Samurai*). In this Western, we have a scene in which the audience first meets Yul Brynner, who will become the leader of the Seven. He's a hired gun at a time when hired guns are no longer being used. Without giving details, suffice it to say he does something reckless and brave, thereby establishing that he is both a decent man and deadly gunman. The next scenes consist of him gathering the rest of the past-their-prime gunmen. Each scene shows us who the person is and what their conflict is, for example, James Coburn is a perfectionist with a gun and a knife, and Robert Vaughn is losing his nerve.

Although there are many variations of first meetings, the basic technique of how to structure the promise is similar and will probably follow one of the models presented above.

First Meetings: The Payoff

While the promise section relies on anticipation, the payoff has a few more weapons at its disposal. The elements that make the first meeting payoff successful are a combination of the following: extraordinary characters, unusual setting, importance of the meeting, compelling dialogue and revealing internal monologue. Not all of these elements must be present (though it would be a hell of a good story if they were), but for this meeting scene to be memorable, at least one must be present and preferably more. It's easy to throw around phrases like "extraordinary characters," but what exactly is meant?

EXTRAORDINARY CHARACTERS

These are characters whose personalities, lifestyles, circumstances and/or professions are fascinating because they are unfamiliar to the average reader. Drop Sammy Glick (from *What Makes Sammy Run?* by Budd Schulberg) in any scene and that scene will be compelling because Sammy's personality is so demanding. The same is true with Sherlock Holmes, Charles Highway (*The Rachel Papers* by Martin Amis), Garp's mother (*The World According to Garp* by John Irving) and Gudrun (*Women in Love* by D.H. Lawrence).

Extraordinary doesn't have to mean flamboyant. It can be an average person, but the difference is that the reader knows this person with such intimacy that he cares for them on a deeper personal level. Holden Caulfield (*The Catcher in the Rye*) is an average kid on many levels (rebellious, angst-filled, self-doubting, self-deluding), but extraordinary in his sensitivity, wit, intelligence and willingness to share his deepest thoughts.

In some cases, extraordinary may simply refer to a person's profession. This is particularly true of minor characters who only have a brief time in the story or scene. Switching the professions of a character from a waiter to someone who changes bulbs on traffic signals heightens the reader's interest because he is learning about something he didn't know anything about. This information is merely a misdirection—increasing the reader's involvement by flashing something shiny at him—while the real purpose of the scene is the character interaction.

UNUSUAL SETTING

This was discussed more fully in chapter five. To quickly recap, sometimes a drab scene can be more interesting and revealing simply by shifting the setting from two characters arguing in a living room to arguing in a theater during a performance of *The King and I*. There's a wonderfully comical scene in the movie *Speechless* in which Michael Keaton and Geena Davis berate each other while supposedly giving a talk to a classroom of school children. They could have had the argument in the hallway, but this setting made it much more clever and funny.

MEETING'S IMPORTANCE

The more important the meeting, the greater the reader's interest. For instance, you could introduce a meeting like this: "Clive hurried through the doors of TransGlobal International determined not to be late the first day of his new job." Obviously, a first day on the job is more important than just any other day on the job. You could complicate it even further: "Clive hurried through the doors of TransGlobal International determined not to be late the first day of his new job. Sure, he wanted a drink—gin, rum, even a lousy light beer—but he couldn't afford to screw up. Not this time—not again. He'd recently found a slip of paper with a phone number in Jenny's car behind the baby seat. When he'd dialed the number, he'd expected it to be a lover, something he could get outraged about and justify another trip to the bar. But it turned out to be one of those divorce attorneys that advertise on TV. That was a week ago. The day of his last drink." Both scenarios promise interesting first meetings with co-workers, bosses and clients. In fact, the opening sentence could have been focused on that aspect: "Clive hurried through the doors of TransGlobal International determined not to be late the first day of his new job. Especially not with this boss, a man with a reputation for firing people for the slightest infraction of company policy. Clive heard that the man had that Nixon-aide Charles Colson's famous saying framed on his office wall: 'Once you have them by the balls, their hearts and minds will follow.'" Although this increases the suspense about the first meeting with this boss, the key element is the stakes. The meeting is important because of the effect it will have on the lives of the characters involved.

COMPELLING DIALOGUE

One of the secrets to compelling dialogue is that the characters don't necessarily have to be talking about something important to the story. A man and woman meet for the first time; the reader sees they are attracted to each other. They don't have to discuss how attracted they are. Instead, they discuss twenty-four-hour restaurants they frequent because they are both insomniacs. This discussion can be much more compelling because it reveals their personalities. Such discussions can be playful, serious or both. Remember that such conversations are not about conveying information, but about building character and momentum.

REVEALING INTERNAL MONOLOGUE

First meetings can be enhanced by one (or more) of the characters reacting to the meeting and revealing his inner self to such an extent that the reader is fascinated. Stanley Elkin's story, "A Poetics for Bullies," creates suspense in meeting the new kid that threatens Push's dominance of his peers. The payoff in this case uses all of the categories mentioned earlier: extraordinary characters, unusual setting, importance of the meeting, compelling dialogue and revealing internal monologue. The scene is too long to reprint here, but I will present the moment that Push first sees his adversary:

"There. See? Do you see him?" Eugene, despite himself, seemed hoarse.

"Be quiet," I said, checking him, freezing as a hunter might. I stared.

He was a Prince, I tell you.

He was tall, tall even sitting down. His long legs comfortable in expensive wool, the trousers of a boy who had been on ships, jets; who owned a horse, perhaps; who knew Latin— what didn't he know?—somebody made up, like a kid in a play with a beautiful mother and a handsome father, who took his breakfast from a sideboard, and picked, even at fourteen and fifteen and sixteen, his mail from a silver plate, he would have hobbies—stamps, stars, things lovely dead. He wore a sport coat, brown as wood, thick as heavy bark. The buttons were leather buds. His shoes seemed carved from horses' saddles, gunstocks. His clothes had grown once in nature. What it must feel like inside those clothes, *I thought.*

I looked at his face, his clear skin, and guessed at the bones, white as bleached wood. His eyes had skies in them. His yellow hair swirled on his head like a crayoned sun.

The power of this passage is in the incredible prose style, which is both vivid and poetic in its imagery. The reader knows from this description that the new kid is an extraordinary character, but the reader also knows that so is Push, because only an extremely intelligent and thoughtful boy would be capable of such a rich and sophisticated description. Within this description, the reader can sense Push's fear and envy of the new kid, all the more powerful because Push doesn't say it directly. Ironically, though this description is part of the payoff, it also manages to increase suspense because now more than ever the reader is anxious to see these two boys confront one another.

Sometimes you may wish to forgo the suspense and merely shout "Surprise!" In such cases, the people in the meeting run into each other without any buildup and the reader experiences the same awkwardness and slight confusion that the characters are going through. The reader may not have any superior knowledge at this point, relying on the information discovered during the dialogue or through one of the character's interior monologues. The sensation for the reader is similar to listening in on a conversation at a neighboring table in a restaurant:

> Stan strolled down the corridor precariously balancing the three-foot stack of quarterly reports he had to read before tomorrow morning's meeting. If he could turn these reports into a brilliant presentation that would win the company some of the Bates fortune, they'd have to make him a partner.
>
> "Hey, Stan. Need a hand?"
>
> Stan peeked over the top of the reports to see Jenny standing there grinning. They'd had two dates already and he was anxious for a third.
>
> "Got it covered, Jen," he said. "But how about tomorrow night? We'll go out and celebrate. We'll get crazy and do something that's illegal in most southern states."
>
> "You're on," she said, winking at him as she turned and hurried back to her desk.
>
> Stan indulged himself, spending a precious fifteen seconds watching her walk. Well worth it, he told himself, rushing to his own office. He walked in, surprised to see one of the firm's partners sitting behind his desk, looking nervous.
>
> "Stan! Stan!" the partner said, standing with open arms as if he were Stan's godfather. "Glad you're back. I'd like you to meet Drew Bates. Drew, this is our best man, Stanley Korbin."
>
> Stan felt his own Adam's apple lodge in his throat.
>
> Drew didn't bother to stand or offer his hand. He just nodded, not even his head. His eyelids. He nodded his eyelids by slowly closing and opening them.
>
> "So?" the partner said brightly. "Ready to give your presentation? Drew has to leave the country tomorrow so he wants to hear your presentation today, in..." The partner glanced at his gold Rolodex. "...Say, twenty minutes."

It appears that the scene is all promise, giving us information about the meeting to come, the stakes and the small amount of time to prepare. The reader is misdirected because having only twenty-four hours is challenge enough, and no one is prepared for the window to be closed to only twenty minutes. Also, the stakes are increased because the reader knows Stan wants a partnership, and this presentation is his ticket. And the pressure is turned up by the nonverbal presence of Drew Bates, the man who is so powerful he doesn't bother to rise or shake hands, but merely nods his eyelids (like a reptile). By giving only this basic information—not even a physical description— the author focuses on Drew as a formidable presence. Adding dialogue or physical description would dilute the impact of the meeting on Stan, and therefore, the reader. Besides, it's implied that since the reader didn't get that information here, he'll get it in the presentation scene, creating more suspense. In this case, the surprise first meeting acts as a type of promise scene for which Stan's presentation in twenty minutes will be the payoff. The scene's function is to raise the questions: Will Stan pull this off? If so, how? The above example emphasizes "the importance of the meeting."

Final Word

It may seem intimidating to think of all the elements that go into making a first meeting scene successful, but it's much easier if you remember that all stories are themselves first meetings between your characters and the reader. Instinctively, you try to make the scenes special in which the reader is first exposed to a character. All you have to do now is treat first meetings between characters the same way. Because the characters have already met in your head, you may forget to include the same sense of spontaneity and wonder that was there when you first thought about them. The techniques discussed above are merely ways to remind you.

❈ 10 ❈

WHEN CHARACTERS COLLIDE:

ACTION &
SUSPENSE SCENES

"I had an interest in death from an early age. It fascinated me. When I heard 'Humpty Dumpty sat on a wall,' I thought, 'Did he fall or was he pushed?'"

P.D. James

"I always begin with character, or characters, and then try to think up as much action for them as possible."

John Irving

Action scenes occur when the conflicting elements of the story, whether they are characters and/or natural forces, collide. A confrontation between these elements must occur to such a degree that at least one character acts with aggression and the other(s) reacts to that aggression. The colliding forces could be nearly anything: an old man versus a marlin (Hemingway's *The Old Man and the Sea*); four men in a lifeboat versus the sea (Stephen Crane's "Open Boat"); a couple of adolescent bullies on a playground (Stanley Elkin's "A Poetics for Bullies"); a woman versus a gang of young children (Joyce Carol Oates's "Naked"); a woman versus a rabid dog (Stephen King's *Cujo*); a woman versus an indifferent, male-dominated organization (films such as *Silkwood, Norma Rae*). The results of these collisions can range from the tame (a heated argument or game of pool) to the apocalyptic (a chainsaw massacre or hundred thousand men shooting at each other on a blood-soaked bat-tlefield). Whatever the scope or however graphic, the writer al-ways wants the reader to be anxious to turn the page and find out what happens next.

Certain stories promise action merely by being within a particular genre: mysteries, Westerns, spy thrillers, horror, men's adventures, war dramas and anything with a shark fin on the cover. The type of action they will deliver is defined by their genre: the mystery will involve murder; the Western will involve shoot-outs; the spy thriller will involve assassinations; horror will involve dismemberment (shark fins belong here); men's adventure will involve big guns; the war drama will in-volve many guns. But these aren't the only kinds of action available. Mainstream stories also have action, sometimes as gruesome and disturbing as any genre story, or even more so since mainstream tends to be more realistic. Russell Banks's *The Sweet Hereafter* has a bus full of school children sinking into icy waters. Herman Melville's *Moby Dick* has a giant whale killing all but one of the novel's characters. Shakespeare's tragedies have a higher body count than *NYPD Blue*. Howev-er, in general, mainstream stories present more subdued ac-tion scenes that don't involve overt violence: characters may merely argue, ignore each other or borrow a sweater. Such scenes can be just as devastating as a fist to the snout because of the effects they have on the characters. This chapter, though, will deal only with the more active and violent action scenes most often found in genre fiction.

An action scene usually has two parts: the promise and the payoff. The promise builds up the *suspense* and the payoff de-livers with the actual *confrontation*. An action movie might open with a group of commandos attacking a terrorist site, but it doesn't start with them shooting. Rather, it shows them sneaking up, checking their watches, signaling each other, tak-ing out the guards. This heightens suspense because the audi-ence gets to know the characters and also knows that the action will continually escalate because something always goes wrong. When something does go wrong—a silent alarm is tripped, a combination lock has been changed—the action part of the scene begins.

However, in longer stories involving several action scenes, these same two categories apply not only to the structure of the individual scene, but also the kind of action scene: *promise-action scene* or *payoff-action scene*.

The Promise-Action Scene

Every story must have suspense of some kind or no one will want to read it. On a basic level, suspense is merely the reader anxious to know what will happen next. The key word here is "anxious." How anxious is the reader to turn the page? Suspense comes from the word "suspend." The more suspense you want to create, the longer you have to *suspend the payoff*. Basically, you're teasing the reader, getting her excited by dangling the Snickers in front of her, then pulling it away. There are two basic dangers with this formula: (1) the longer you suspend the payoff, the greater the risk of losing reader interest; and (2) the longer you suspend the payoff, the more satisfying that payoff must be. There's no magic formula for avoiding those dangers, but being aware of them and rereading suspense scenes with them in mind will help.

The effectiveness of the action scene depends to a large extent on the level of suspense you've created prior to the action. The job of the promise-action scene is to create suspense through anticipation—in essence, to hype the forthcoming payoff-action scene the way film trailers hype upcoming movies. It promises that even better action scenes will follow. Remember, though, that *the promise-action scene is also an action scene*. It must contain some action that is appropriate to the genre. Its function is to give the reader a taste of the action that is to come, yet not be so active or elaborate that the payoff scene can't top it. If you have a jewel heist story, the first jewel heist scene can't be more clever, dangerous or complex than the climactic jewel heist, otherwise the rest of the story will be a letdown. The action must build in steady increments, each action scene satisfying in itself, yet more intense than the preceding one.

Nearly each episode of *The X-Files* begins with a promise-action scene: something horrible happens to someone who is not the main character. Then the main characters, Scully and

Mulder, come in to investigate. This introduces the conflict, e.g., flesh-eating insects who can scurry out of toilet bowls. Many suspense novels begin the same way, focusing on a "throwaway victim" rather than main characters. The purpose of this opening scene is to establish the *stakes*. Just as with poker, the level of interest and suspense increase with the amount of the stakes. In an opening promise-action scene like this, the writer has two elements to adjust the level of stakes: (1) how much we care about or are fascinated by the throwaway victim, and (2) the intensity level of the action/violence.

The term "throwaway victim" may be misleading. Beginning writers make the mistake of thinking that because this character is going to die in the first scene, the reader shouldn't get too close to him or her. As a result, such writers will create only the sketchiest of character types. However, they should do the exact opposite. The richer the characterization of throwaway victims, the closer the reader gets, the more she feels the shock of loss when they are killed, and, therefore, the higher the stakes. The reader now has a personal interest in seeing the killer brought down. Plus, you're telling the reader that during the course of the story, any character could die, no matter how much you like them, which increases the suspense. Following is the opening of the prologue (promise-action scene) from the novel I just finished, *Assassin's Apprentice*:

> *It had taken Brett Stuart his entire senior year of high school to get Karla Easton alone and there was no way he was leaving this meadow today without somehow touching her breasts. One or both, left or right, direct fondle or accidental brush, it didn't matter. It* would *happen. He had a foolproof plan.*
>
> *"You find any yet?" Karla called from over by the oak tree.*
>
> *"Nope. Nothing yet." Brett pretended to look all around him for a hemp plant, though he knew none grew here. That was the devious beauty of his plan. He rustled a few scraggly weeds for effect.*
>
> *"Man, I'm burning up out here," she said. "I wish I'd thought to pack some Gatorade. How you holding up, Brett? Need some more sunscreen?"*
>
> *"I'm fine," he replied, wishing she'd stop being so damn*

thoughtful. He looked at his watch. They'd been out here two hours already. If he didn't make his big move soon, they'd both go home empty-handed.

"Hey, I think I found one," Karla said, but her voice was more hopeful than certain.

"Really? Let me see." Brett jogged across the field, not too fast because when he ran his thick lumpish body fell into the girlish waddle that he was always being teased about in gym class. One of the many things he was always teased about. Christ, where would the list begin? His weight, his overbite, his thick Mr. Peepers glasses, the dark purple birthmark on his cheek that looked like a June bug squashed against a windshield. He was a walking catalogue of every outcast mannerism or physical oddity that tattooed loser status on a kid. He had a wheezing laugh, a nasal voice, and the clothes—he shook his head woefully as he ran—don't get me started on these sissy clothes my mother picked out of a goddamn Spiegel catalogue. This isn't Philadelphia, he'd told her, it's godforsaken Wyoming! Her icy reply was always the same: "Good taste is not geographical."

"What have...you got there...Karla?" he asked, wheezing as he ran up to her.

"Johansson's private stash, I hope. This look like hemp?" She pointed to a cluster of weeds circling the tree. She had scissors in one hand and a plastic baggie in the other. "It looks like the photograph in the book. I think."

Brett pretended to examine the plant carefully, not wanting to hurt her feelings for making such an obvious mistake. Not even close. "Good guess, Karla. Very, very close. But the leaves of the Cannabis sativa are serrated, like a bread knife. See, these aren't. They're more scalloped than serrated."

"Damn, what is wrong with me? I know that. Duh!" She smiled at him, teeth straight and milk-fed white. "Sorry, Brett. I'll try harder. I promise." She shoved the scissors and baggie in opposite hip pockets and wandered off through the meadow. She wore bib overalls and a long-sleeved T-shirt and walked bent over so she could better examine the plants. He could see her breasts bounce slightly against the denim bib. Not bounce so much as bob. Her breasts weren't especially large (his own *were probably bigger), but they were here and he'd never touched any before. He doubted he'd ever even been breast-fed; his mother wouldn't have stood for the mess.*

He leaned up against the oak tree and watched Karla diligently zig-zagging through the weeds. Her apple-scented shampoo lingered and Brett inhaled deeply, hoovering every last particle. For God's sake, what was he thinking? She was a sweet and trusting girl who'd come to him for some help and here he was like those drooling Neanderthals from school, scheming to dehumanize and humiliate her. He punched his thigh hard. Pain burned down to his kneecap. He punched himself again and the thigh went icy numb. That helped.

Brett looked around. Thought he'd heard something. He wasn't sure what. Something. A rapid ticking followed by a screeching zing, like a guitar string snapping. A bird maybe, or insect. "Karla?"

"Huh?"

"You hear something?"

The line "You hear something?" introduces the suspense element and is the beginning of the actual action of the scene. After this, they are chased by an unknown, unseen being— we'll get to that in a moment. First, let's dissect what we have so far. I start with misdirection, a technique discussed in several previous chapters. The misdirection is a minisuspense element: Will Brett touch Karla's breasts? That question is posed in the opening paragraph so while the reader reads on to find out whether or not he succeeds, I try to create more complex characters than the reader first assumed were here. Yes, he wants to cop a feel, but not because he's like all the other guys at school—rather because he's the opposite. Nor is she a simple cheerleading bimbo; she's good in school, kind to him, a decent person. She doesn't deserve to be exploited, as if he could, which he realizes and punishes himself for even thinking. The fact that he is in such a desperate romantic place, plus the fact that he punishes himself makes us like him more. Also, it's clear that he's very smart, an element that I introduce as a hope for him to escape the thing that will eventually be after them. In addition, I introduce a *false conflict*: his problems with his too-strict parents (you have a description of his mother, and one about the moral inflexibility of his father follows the scene you've read). This is a false conflict because the reader assumes that since it's been brought up, it will somehow tie into the story, perhaps even be resolved. Not so.

Now that I've introduced the "You hear something?" hook, which every reader knows means something nasty is coming, I have the characters ignore it. This heightens the suspense. The reader is thinking, "What is that thing? Where is it? Get the hell out of there!" But the characters go on oblivious to the danger. At this point, I, too, ignore the suspense/plot conflict and return to the character conflict: how Brett feels about Karla. In this way, I'm writing as if it were a mainstream story about Brett confronting his hopeless romantic fantasies and coming to some self-realizations about himself. We'll skip ahead a few pages. He's recounting how he lured her to this field so they could be alone:

> *Then what, dummy?*
>
> *She'd forget your girlish waddle and deviated septum and boorish personality and rip open her blouse and beg you to please touch them, kiss them hard, Butt Gut? What would she say if she knew he had a keepsake of hers in his school backpack? One afternoon he'd watched her and a couple of her girlfriends leaving school after track practice. Her hair was wet and straight from a shower and it kept glinting sunlight at him. He followed like a fish follows a sparkling lure. He saw them sneak a cigarette at the McDonald's. They passed it around laughing as each took a couple puffs, knowing the coach would kill them if she saw them. They stubbed it out on the sidewalk outside, where Brett retrieved it. Now he kept it in the snakebite kit his mother made him carry in his backpack ("It's Wyoming, dear, where the animals don't yet know their place"). Sometimes he took it out and stared at the three different lipstick shades, pleased with himself for being able to pick out Karla's. A demure Peach Nectar.*
>
> *"Ow!" Karla's voice yelped. He looked around but couldn't see her.*
>
> *"Karla?"*
>
> *"Ow! Shit, that hurts!"*

> *"Karla, where are you?"*
> *"By the creek."*
> *"You okay?"*
> *"Yeah. Kinda. Something weird just happened."*
>
> Brett waded through the chest-high weeds and around a thicket of brush until he came to the grassy banks of the creek. Karla was kneeling by the water wringing out the white scrunchie she'd taken from her ponytail. She pressed the wet cloth against one eye. He pulled the scrunchie away. The skin around her eye was puffy and red, as if she'd been slapped. And the eye itself was no longer blue like the other one, but a yellowish-gold. The sight of it turned his stomach sour. *"Jesus, what happened?"*
>
> *"I don't know, really. I was just kneeling here, looking at plants. Suddenly I had this sharp pain."*

Notice how the story segues from his self-analysis to something concrete: Karla's holler for help. Nothing much has happened, just something stinging her eye, until he sees that her eye has changed to an unnatural color. It's something small, but it *promises* that something bigger is coming. So far there are two parallel sets of questions the reader is asking. One has to do with the suspense plot: What was the sound they heard? What caused her eye to turn that color? Will Brett and Karla survive? The second involves their characters: What will Karla and Brett's personal relationship be like after this? Will Brett break away from his parents?

That's a lot of questions. The questions create the suspense; the payoff portion of the scene fulfills the promise.

The Payoff-Action Scene

The second element that creates stakes is the intensity level of the violence, which directly reflects on how much we want the villain to get caught. This element is the realm of the payoff-action scene. The revenge genre is a perfect example. Have you ever found yourself watching a perfectly dreadful cable movie that you keep intending to turn off but you can't because you just want to see the rotten bastard of a villain get his just desserts? To create this desire, the villain has to do something

✓ so horrible that it outrages the audience. Clint Eastwood, Charles Bronson and Bruce Willis have made careers out of exacting this revenge. To achieve this level of outrage, the opening action scene must have a high level of violence. This can be achieved three ways:

- ✦ through numbers—instead of just one person being killed, an entire building is blown up.
- ✦ through the type of victim—innocent people, especially children who are harmed, raise the reader's sympathetic emotions.
- ✦ through the amount of graphic detail of the violence—the more horrible the type of pain, the more the reader is obsessed with chasing after the killer. The killer who uses a knife to eviscerate his victim is more awful than the one who merely shoots his victims.

Of course, regarding the third element, there is a point of diminishing returns. You have crossed this point when the act of violence is so horrible that the reader loses interest in the victim. For example, when William Goldman was hired to write the screenplay for Stephen King's *Misery*, he insisted on following the book in writing the famous hobbling scene. In the book, Paul (the writer) tries to escape from Annie (his crazed fan), so she takes an ax and propane torch and cuts off his feet. To Goldman, this was a "moment": "I knew I had to write the movie. That scene would linger in audiences' memories as I knew it would linger in mine." But Goldman ran into problems. First, Warren Beatty, who was interested in playing Paul, advised him that if they cut off the feet, the audience would look at Paul as a loser. Goldman disagreed. Goldman went on vacation and returned to find that director Rob Reiner and one of the producers had tightened the script—as well as changed the amputation scene. Instead of cutting off the feet, Annie breaks them with a sledgehammer. Goldman was livid, screaming at everyone involved. "And you know what?" he admitted in his introduction to the published screenplay. "I was wrong.... If we had gone the way I wanted, it would have been too much. The audience would have hated

Kathy [Bates] and, in time, hated us."

You might ask, if it wasn't too violent for the book, why was it for the film? First, since a film is a more aggressive art form, there's no retreating from the images. With a book, you can pace yourself, stop when you want. But with a film, the gruesome images just keep rolling. Second, maybe it was too violent for the book. Despite the fact that it was a best-seller and King is a remarkable writer, perhaps that scene did make the reader care less about Paul. I wrote a series of action novels called *The Warlord* under the name Jason Frost. Brief premise summary: A doomsday earthquake breaks California off from the U.S.; a meltdown of nuclear reactors causes an inversion layer like a bowl over the island of California so no one can leave or come in. Those who are still in the state must fight for survival. One group of bad guys kidnaps women into slavery, shaving their heads and pulling all of their teeth. The hero's wife was among the women and he was out to rescue her. When a woman friend of mine read this in manuscript form, she complained that as soon as she'd read the scene in which the wife's teeth are yanked out, she lost interest in seeing her rescued. I realized she was right. As much as I'd liked the writing in that scene, I did away with the teeth removal and just left them with shaved heads.

Let's return to that prologue of my novel, *Assassin's Apprentice*. Above I discussed how I constructed the promise. In the payoff scene, Karla and Brett see two figures in contamination suits spraying a chemical on the field. Not wanting to get caught trespassing, they flee but run into something hideous that makes Karla scream and Brett wet his pants. (Like a good monster movie, I don't describe what they see in this scene; *that* payoff comes later.) Karla is frozen in terror, so Brett takes her hand and forces her to run. She trips and starts crawling on all fours like a feral animal. Brett tries to keep up, but when he turns to see if they're being followed, he feels the same sting in his eye that Karla described. Suddenly, he too starts crawling, with surprising physical power:

> *He crashed through the weeds like a locomotive, surprised at his own power and speed. His movements were smooth and*

athletic in a way he never was while standing on his feet, balancing all that lumpish weight. His barrel body churned through the weeds so fluidly he felt like a fish darting through tropical waters. For the first time in his life Brett didn't hate his body. He now knew the elation the other boys must feel when they ran a touchdown, finger-rolled a layup, blasted a home run. How Karla must feel when she won a race. Mastery over time and space. A flash of holy grace.

Suddenly something had a tight hold of his ankle and Brett's forward movement sent him sprawling face-first into the dirt like a speared frog. Terrified, he tried to kick his foot free and claw his way forward with his broken and bleeding fingernails. The grip on his ankle seemed to loosen and his body tingled with hope. One more lunge...

Then something snagged his other ankle too and he was flipped over onto his back like a turtle. Fat and powerless once again.

Three figures in tinfoil astronaut suits stood beside him. They all had those tinted helmets, weird binocular visors and spray guns. The bottom half of their black-tinted helmets had some kind of data projected on it, like a computer screen. The data kept shifting between words and charts and maps. One of the astronauts held Brett's ankles up in the air, which he now dropped. "Where is it, son?" one of them asked calmly. Brett couldn't tell which one because the voice was electronically broadcast from a microphone inside the helmet. Brett relaxed, they were here to help. He tried to describe the thing he and Karla had seen, to warn them, but his excitement made the saliva splash around his mouth and he stuttered and sprayed garbled syllables as he had during the state spelling bee when he was nine. It had cost him the championship. Garbonzo, so simple.

One of them, the one who had held his ankles, suddenly kicked Brett hard in the hip. "Goddamn it, where!" she demanded, her angry voice booming from the speakers on her helmet. Her anger seemed to invoke a flurry of new data scrolling across her helmet. Again Brett tried to speak, but again it came out mush. Frustrated, he pushed himself to his knees and pointed furiously over his shoulder toward where they had just run *from. But in midgesture he felt a cool mist against his face and he crumbled to the ground. Garbonzo: G-A-R....*

And that ends the chapter. Brett and Karla are "throwaway victims," existing only to establish stakes and introduce the antagonist. Everything that happens in the above section is for a purpose:

1. At first they see someone in a funky contamination suit. This tells the reader something bad is going on in this area, which is described earlier in the chapter as being deserted and off-limits to residents. Also, while the reader is looking at the left hand (the person in the suit), I can use the right hand to bring in the real threat—the thing that chases them.

2. Brett wets his pants. That tells us that whatever he's looking at—which I don't show the reader until later in the novel—is truly frightening.

3. Despite his fear, he grabs Karla's hand and tries to protect her. He finds the hero within him, which makes the reader remember why she likes him and roots for him to survive.

4. Brett has the same mysterious eye thing happen to him. This reminds the reader that the eye stinging is significant and related to whatever is chasing them.

5. My favorite passage in the chapter is the paragraph that begins, "He crashed through the weeds like a locomotive, surprised at his own power and speed" and ends with, "For the first time in his life Brett didn't hate his body. He now knew the elation the other boys must feel.... A flash of holy grace." I spent several days on this paragraph because it's a moment of revelation for Brett. He came to the field to touch Karla's breast but instead does something heroic and experiences the depths of grace, athletic and spiritual. Again, this cranks up the suspense because the reader wants him to survive, but it also completes the character arc on his internal conflicts, thereby not treating him as just a throwaway victim.

6. When the people in the foil suits capture him, the reader relaxes a bit because she thinks he's safe now. Then the

woman kicks him and the reader is startled back to fear. The woman is later revealed to be a major character in the novel, so this scene immediately establishes what kind of person she is. There's an old screenwriter's maxim: When the hero first appears on screen, he must kiss a baby; when the villain first appears, he must kick a dog. That's not to be taken literally, although Stephen King does it in *The Dead Zone* when his villain kicks a dog to death. And I'm not too far behind having my villain kick the puppy-like Brett.

7. Finally, the spelling bee reference adds a sadness to Brett's death: Not only are they killing him, but even worse, he reverts back to the clumsy, insecure kid he was before his revelation. This makes us mourn him more deeply and hate them more.

Even though this was the payoff portion of the scene—involving chasing and killing—the scene itself is a promise scene. It promises (1) to tell you why their eyes turned gold, (2) what was chasing them, (3) who the people in the foil suits are and (4) why they had to kill the kids.

"You Put Your Right Fist In, You Pull His Right Ear Off"

Action scenes often involve violent one-on-one combat. Describing such action is not as easy as you might think. Beginning writers often merely "block" the scene, which is what stage directors do when they tell the actors where to move and stand. This creates a static scene of characters moving and acting robotically.

The most important rule when writing an action scene is to not lose sight of the characters. Remember, it's not the action that's important; it's who's doing the action that we care about. You have to continue to emphasize the characters while they are in the action. This is accomplished by focusing on their internal monologue and external dialogue.

The second rule of writing action scenes is descriptive detail. How you go about describing action depends upon your style preferences. Some writers prefer very plain, straightforward prose; others like a richer, more poetic style.

The following excerpt from *Assassin's Apprentice* involves the two main heroes, Harper and Thomas, against three thugs, Gregory, Donner and Axel, who were hired to kill Harper. Harper is the woman sheriff of a tiny Wyoming town; Thomas is a professional assassin come to help her out of a serious situation. We're starting halfway through the chapter. The thugs had been sitting at the bar of this small-town restaurant drinking beer and waiting for the right moment to move against Harper. Unexpectedly, the owner, Marla, serves them three beers sent over by Thomas. They're confused, since they don't know him. All they know is that he's sitting with the woman they're going to kill. Also, the entire time Thomas has been sitting with Harper, he's been building some bizarre sculpture made out of silverware and plates. The killers approach Thomas and ask why he bought them beer, to which Thomas cryptically replies, "To bring you over here." The leader of the trio, Axel, pulls a gun and puts it to Thomas's forehead. Harper goes for her gun, but gets pistol-whipped by Gregory, leaving her dazed on the floor; she becomes no more than a narrator of the following action. The killers then proceed to shoot the bartender, Marla, and a customer, threatening to shoot the others in the place—and you can tell they will enjoy it. Axel reins them in, barking orders, until:

Thomas, who'd never looked up during the shootings, now glanced up at Axel. The two men exchanged a look that Harper's throbbing brain tried to interpret. Axel seemed somehow startled, perhaps even scared by what he saw in Thomas's face. And she could see that angered him. Thomas, however, merely looked sad. When he spoke it was with a surprising gentleness, almost compassion. "The problem with you boys is you like your work too much. You take pleasure in the act itself rather than in the completion of the job. That's the difference between instant gratification and delayed gratification—the difference between animals and humans. In delayed gratification lies the principle of salvation."

"What the fuck's he talkin' about?" Donner said. "Shoot the fucker."

"I'm talking about how you should have shot her first." He

pointed at Harper. "Then me. Then just left. The rest of this..." he waved a dismissive hand around the room, "...is just sloppiness. You've got to learn to keep your eyes on the prize."

Axel, as if in defiance, swung his gun away from Thomas and jammed it against Harper's cheek. Out of the corner of her eye Harper could see Axel's finger tighten on the trigger. She felt like encouraging him: Yes, do it, already. End it.

But then Thomas moved. Harper was still groggy, and what she witnessed next happened so fast she couldn't be sure she was seeing it accurately.

Thomas pounded his fist on the spoon wedged under the salt shaker, which flipped the salad bowl two feet in the air above the table. The silverware flew up too. Axel, Gregory and Donner watched the flying plate and silverware, distracted for a moment by the unexpected display of soaring tableware. Harper thought Donner was even smiling, like a kid at a magic show.

With one hand, Thomas snatched a knife from midair and plunged it into Axel's chest. With the other hand, he snagged the falling knife and leaped up at Axel, jamming the knife into Axel's throat. While he was slicing through Axel's windpipe, he yanked Axel's gun from his hand and shot Donner through the head. Donner fell over. Like some macabre ventriloquist with his dummy, Thomas maneuvered Axel's body around by the knife handle sticking out of his neck. While Axel clutched desperately at the bloody weapon, trying to pull it free, Thomas shoved him into Gregory, who was aiming his gun at Thomas. The gun went off, ripping a chunk of flesh from Axel's side. Axel tried to yell in pain, but the effort only resulted in blood gurgling from the slice in his throat. The baby turned toward the familiar sound of gurgling and began excitedly to jump up and down on his father's lap.

Thomas continued ramming Axel's body into Gregory, until all three men tumbled to the ground.

Harper had recovered her senses enough to pull her own gun out and launch herself from the chair. But the instant she stood up, her legs folded under her and she fell to the ground, her head spinning. Blood dripped into her eyes, which she frantically swiped with her fingers. Clutching her gun with both *hands, she crawled toward Thomas, determined to help him. By the time she got close enough for her blurry eyesight to distinguish bodies, she saw Thomas astride Gregory's chest like kids in a playground fight. Except Thomas had a gun pressed against Gregory's forehead.*

Gregory pleaded, "No, please, please!"

Thomas looked around, grabbed a plastic-coated menu and held it over Gregory's face. He looked at Harper and said, "Turn away. This will be messy."

"What?" Harper said dully, not turning away.

Gregory, bucking uselessly under Thomas, continued to beg. "For God's sake, please. I mean it, man. I'm sorry, I didn't—"

Thomas fired twice through the menu and into Gregory's skull. The plastic menu caught most of the splash of blood, skull and brains. Some erupted to the side, peppering Harper's face. She accepted the baptism without flinching.

"Well," Thomas said, rising, tossing the menu aside. "It's started." He held out a hand for Harper. "Come on, we've a lot to do before your cop pals arrive."

The challenge during such a scene is that the reader knows our heroes aren't going to be killed because then the novel would be over. So the suspense question isn't, "Will they be killed?" but rather, "How will they get out of it?" Therefore, to increase suspense, you have to focus on making the heroes' escape more difficult. The following notes discuss why I made certain choices within the scene.

1. Having Thomas spook the killers by buying them a round of beer catches the reader by surprise as much as it does the killers. For the first part of the chapter, they're just waiting for them to attack. Now the reader knows Thomas is on to them and wonders what he'll do about it since we know he's not carrying a gun. Yes, he could have warned Harper, but he knows she wouldn't do anything based on his hunch. Plus, he's a bit of a burnout, more interested in the challenge of disposing of them as the necessity.

2. The silverware and plate sculpture is a suspense device. The reader doesn't know why he's doing this odd thing,

but soon she sees its purpose.

3. "To bring you over here." This should hike up the anticipation a notch because Thomas brought them over for a reason. Why would he bring three armed killers to his table?

4. Axel pulls out his gun and this begins the actual action portion of the scene—the payoff. Immediately, stakes are established by a series of actions: the gun against Thomas's head, the pistol-whipping of Harper (which also serves to temporarily remove her access to her gun, leaving the heroes completely unarmed), the shooting of the bartender and customer. This is the cliff-hanging device: increasing the threat (in this case, the nastiness of the villains) while decreasing the options of the heroes.

5. The paragraph that describes the bartender, Marla, being shot is crucial. (In the description, Marla just stands there for a minute, looking surprised. She looks down at her chest, sees the blood, touches the seeping hole and says, "Jesus, why'd you do that?" Then she drops to the ground.) I wanted it to be mundane rather than melodramatic. Instead of the cinematic cliché of a huge, gaping hole and the body thrown backward, I went with the more realistic description. Also, I wanted the moment to be a little sad (the reader gets to know her character in the first part of the chapter) for three reasons: (1) to crank up the reader's desire for revenge and, therefore, the suspense; (2) to show that the killers are ruthless and will kill without hesitation; and (3) to show that Thomas, though a hero, is also a bit callous by not reacting.

6. As I said above, the challenge in maintaining suspense is that the reader knows the heroes won't be killed this early, but she doesn't know about some of the minor characters. Earlier in the chapter I introduced a young couple and their baby sitting at a back table. Now that the reader sees the killers shoot two other minor characters, she is worried for this family. The reader doesn't know if they'll survive, but she wants them to. This increases suspense because it puts pressure on the heroes not just to survive, which the reader already assumes they will, but to save this family. The wife is pregnant, just to add to the stakes.

7. "Thomas, who'd never looked up during the shootings, now glanced up at Axel." This paragraph is key because it defines the action scene as being about more than the action itself. The fact that Thomas never looked up during the shootings indicates what a burnout he is, how removed from compassion he is. This is important because the novel is in part about Thomas's redemption of his humanity through helping Harper. It's the reason he comes to her aid. This moment shows how far he has to go.

   In addition, the reader sees that Thomas recognizes some part of himself in the killers, which is why there's a gentleness in his voice when he addresses them. And what he tells them about delayed gratification is indeed the essence of all religious teaching, which establishes some degree of intellect in his character.

   Finally, in the next few paragraphs, the reader realizes that what Thomas is saying—aside from its truth—is also a ploy for him to attack. He's maneuvering them into position.

8. When the gun is put to Harper's head, instead of the typical hero's defiance, she almost welcomes the end. The previous pages help the reader understand her feelings. This is part of her character arc: to come out from under the shadow of both her father and grandfather, and gain confidence in herself as a separate person.

9. When Thomas pounds his fist on the spoon, sending his sculpture of silverware into the air, this signifies what the reader has been waiting for: the counteraction (the hero overcoming impossible odds). I'm well aware that this method is unconventional, but that's what I like about it. I had the idea for this scene for years before I found the right book to put it in. I knew it would be hard to pull off because the reader could find it to be too gimmicky and that would kill the tone of the scene, but what I like about it is that it's like a magic trick (and a writing trick): distract with one hand while manipulating with the other. The thugs watch him piling his silverware, but do nothing because it doesn't look like weapons when balanced together like artwork.

The description of the actual killing that follows is brief, to the point, matter-of-fact. I want to show that Thomas is even more ruthless than they are.

I like the baby getting excited at Axel's gurgling. It reminds us of the other characters in the room, but it also gives the moment a sickening irony—the idea that violence breeds violence.

10. Harper recovers from her pistol-whipping enough to pull her gun and try to help. But she's still too groggy. This sets the reader up for her still being disoriented when Thomas tells her to turn her head because he's about to shoot the pleading Gregory in the face. I want the reader to be in Harper's point of view for this moment to experience the complete ruthlessness of his action.

11. Finally, in the last paragraph, Thomas tells Harper that "it's started," meaning that the real villain has sent killers and things are only going to get worse. But he's also telling her that she's going to have to cross a line now: She's going to have to help concoct a lie to tell her own deputies when they arrive. If she wants to survive, she'll have to step over from a belief in law and order into the shadowy world of gray morality that Thomas lives in. The chapter ends there because that's the hook: Will she do it or will she insist on telling the truth as she has in the past?

The McGuffin

In general, both mystery and suspense novels rely on action scenes to increase suspense and pay off the reader's patience. The difference between the two genres is that the mystery novel starts with a body and the rest of the novel is about figuring out who the killer is and why the murder took place. The suspense novel may or may not have a mystery within it, such as who the top villain is or why some grand scheme was carried off in the beginning, but at its heart it's mostly one big chase scene. The heroes are after something and the villains are chasing them so they don't get it. What is the thing they're after? Hitchcock called it the McGuffin, meaning that it doesn't matter all that much because the audience is interested in the chase itself. This doesn't mean you shouldn't work to come up with an intriguing, original McGuffin. Certainly that would enhance your story quite a bit. But keep your focus on what the payoff of the genre is for the reader: the excitement of the chase.

In the best suspense novels, there are two types of McGuffins: (1) The *big goal* is the plot McGuffin. The secret formula that turns water into fuel. The hidden artwork stolen by the Nazis. Government secrets. The lost ark. Whatever it is, the person who possesses it will have great wealth or power over others. (2) The *intimate goal* focuses on the effect the search has on the characters. In William Goldman's *Marathon Man*, the big goal is diamonds stolen by Nazis from murdered Jews. The intimate goal is Babe coming out from his self-imposed emotional imprisonment due to his father's suicide. The parallel is that the diamonds were taken from Jews trying to escape the concentration camps, while Babe has locked himself up because of the persecution of his father during the McCarthy Communist witch-hunts. Yes, there are many satisfying action scenes, but the most satisfying payoff is Babe coming into his own on a personal level.

How About Them Villains?

The villains in the above scene are minor "throwaway villains," meaning their sole purpose is to die, but to die in such a way as to elevate suspense. This is accomplished in two ways: (1) The reader knows that the next killers sent will be much more professional and deadly, so she anxiously anticipates them, wondering how the heroes will escape them. (2) The reader has seen how ruthless Thomas is, which makes her look forward to meeting the major villain. In a lengthy suspense novel like this one, there are several layers of villains. In fact, there are at least ten villains in *Assassin's Apprentice*. Each is like a barrier that the heroes must get through in order to finally get to the head villain. That means that each confrontation gets harder and more dangerous. As the villains get tougher, so does the toll on the heroes. In this novel, they both suffer losses of friends and family as well as considerable physical wounds. On the mental level, as Thomas becomes more and more humane, Harper actually becomes more and more ruthless, until finally, although the big goal is to save the world, the intimate goal is to save each other's humanity.

On a practical level, when you have so many villains, you are faced with the problem of how to kill them off. Writers sometimes kill off the villains in a mundane way, leaving the reader feeling cheated. You can't make the reader hate these characters so intensely over hundreds of pages, only to have them get shot once and drop dead. Each must die, but each death must be progressively harder to achieve than the last, and preferably more horrible for the next villain than the last. There are two ways to achieve this: ever-increasing physical pain or psychic pain.

In the first method, each death is physically more elaborate than the last. The first villain is shot and dies. The second is burned alive and runs screaming across the lawn. The next is slowly lowered into a vat of acid/piranhas/leeches, writhing as the extremities are gnawed away. Of course, the worst demise is saved for the last, most important villain. A few years ago, impaling was popular. Every movie involved impaling of some kind. Many writers prefer the popular but corny "poetic justice" death in which the villain attacks the hero with a knife (or some other weapon) and ends up getting stabbed by his own weapon. For me, such a clichéd ending is always a disappointment because it's a sign that the writer couldn't come up with anything clever. The problem with this method is that it can easily become cartoonish, as it did in the film *The Long Kiss Goodnight*. The characters get lost in service to the ever-increasing stunts.

The second way to achieve the horrible end for the villain is to hurt them on a mental level. That is, you take away something they want more than the McGuffin. In some cases, this could mean that a family member or romantic interest whom they deeply love is inadvertently or deliberately destroyed as a result of the villain's actions. In most cases, this involves pride, specifically how they think of themselves. For some villains, defeat is worse than death. Not just on the competitive level, but on the artistic level. Imagine the villain as an artist whose scheme is his artwork. The destruction of that scheme is like slashing the Mona Lisa to ribbons in front of da Vinci. In such a case, the actual death of the villain is secondary to having destroyed his essence. In *Assassin's Apprentice*, Cooper is a particularly cold-blooded villain. Before she is finally caught, the reader has witnessed her killing characters from innocent teenagers to the hero's grandfather. She's baaad! Earlier in the novel, there's a scene during which she has lunch with her sister, who's a nun. Much of Cooper's life has been a direct reaction to the oppressive goodness of her sister. In this scene, Cooper has the heroes, Thomas and Harper, trapped in a house, which she sets on fire. Harper and Thomas manage to escape and capture her. She's lying on the ground after giving them the information they want.

> *Cooper looked past Harper and Thomas, staring at the flames whipping through the house. She stared at it as if admiring a sculpture in a museum. She smiled brightly. "You ever hear of Saint Agnes?"*
>
> *"Patron saint of virgins," Thomas said. He pressed his gun under her chin.*
>
> *Cooper smiled. "Also of Girl Scouts, which everyone probably assumes are virgins. In 304, when she was thirteen, she had all these wealthy Roman suitors pursuing her. But she turned them all down, including the governor's son. She tells them, 'I have chosen a spouse who cannot be seen with mortal eyes, whose mouth drips with milk and honey.' Meaning, of course, Jesus. Though it's kind of a drooling Jesus if you ask me. Anyway, the governor offers her all these riches to marry his son, and threatens to torture her to death if she refuses. Naturally, she refuses. So, he strips her naked in order to parade her through the streets. She's unimpressed, declaring, 'You will see that my God is a God of purity. He will bring your wicked purpose to naught.' Hell, I'd've roasted her ass just for using the word 'naught.' But that's me. So, he marches her naked self through the streets, but miraculously her blonde hair suddenly grows so long it hides her nudity. Still, he dumps her off in a brothel in order to shame her more. Then in the brothel, the first customer to step up for a helping of Agnes pie is the governor's son, who is immediately struck blind. But being the saintly type, Agnes cures him. Nevertheless, the governor sends her to*

> *be burned at the stake. They say she marched to that stake more cheerfully than most women march to their weddings." Cooper stopped, looked at Harper. "Quite a role model, huh? Better than Malibu Barbie."*
>
> *Harper just stared, perplexed by Cooper's speech.*
>
> *And suddenly Cooper bolted. But she wasn't running away from them, she wasn't trying to escape. She was running toward the house. Thomas lowered his gun to his side and watched Cooper dive through the window that she had tossed the grenades through earlier. She landed right into the thickest nest of flames. When she stood up, her clothes were already patched with flames. But she made no attempt to pat them out. She faced Thomas and Harper and smiled as the fire ran up her blouse and leaped to her hair, which whooshed into one bright flame. She stared defiantly without making a sound until the fire fully engulfed her. She fell to the floor out of sight. Harper was amazed that Cooper had been able to stand as long as she did.*
>
> *Thomas lowered his gun and marched to the patrol car without looking back. "Let's go. We have to stop at an all-night store."*

Cooper has already lost everything, so for the heroes to kill her would be a letdown, no matter how gruesome her death was. But this death is oddly fascinating because it completes the character arc started earlier when the reader saw her competitive resentment of her sister. Her death is a mockery of martyrdom and a comment on her own self-loathing. Since the reader couldn't possibly hate her anymore, I wanted to nudge that hatred into something surprising: pity.

Final Word

There are as many different kinds of action scenes as there are actions. The examples given in this chapter are only a sampling. Remember that a novel may contain many action scenes, but you have to be careful not to repeat yourself or any of the other action scenes you've read or seen. Otherwise the scenes will be predictable and lose any excitement.

WHAT'S SO FUNNY?
COMIC SCENES

> *"Good taste and humour are a contradiction in terms, like a chaste whore."*
> Malcolm Muggeridge

> *"The strongest should come first in comedy because once a character is really established as funny everything he does becomes funny."*
> F. Scott Fitzgerald

> *"The world is a comedy to those that think; a tragedy to those that feel."*
> Horace Walpole

A comic once said, "Dying is easy. Comedy is hard." Anyone who tries to write comic scenes will soon learn the painful truth of this statement. The biggest problem, of course, is defining what's funny. What one person thinks is knee-slapping hilarious, another will find jaw-dropping offensive. Some people love Jim Carrey's crazy antics while others stare stone-faced, asking, "What's everybody laughing at?" *There's Something About Mary* was a big comedy hit in 1999, yet many people walked out of the film in disgust. Since it's nearly impossible to please everyone, the comedy writer is better off just pleasing herself. If *you* think it's funny, go with that. However, be aware that even if you're good at telling a joke or making people laugh around the water cooler, that may not translate into being funny on the page. Just as the class clown has to go to actual clown school to be a professional, there are some techniques and tips to get the most out of your humor.

Almost all fiction, even the darkest stories, contain some

humor. Shakespeare's grimmest tragedies have scenes that feature slapstick, bawdy jokes and outrageous situations. *Moby Dick* has a funny chapter in which narrator Ishmael discovers he's sharing a bed with a headhunter. *The Catcher in the Rye* is about a teenager having a nervous breakdown, yet it is one of the funniest novels ever written. In fact, it would be very difficult to find a tragic story that didn't offer periodic humor. The reason for this is quite practical: A dark story can depress the reader to the point that he loses interest. People can stare only so long into the bitter heart of human misery before they have to turn away. Humor in such stories gives the reader a respite from the intensity. If the story is unrelentingly dark, a tragic ending may make the reader relieved that everyone—including himself—is finally out of their misery. Occasional humor makes the loss seem greater, the tragedy even more tragic.

Humor also makes the reader care more about the characters. It's pretty much the same as in real life. People who are stern and humorless aren't much fun to be around. They seem to lack a balanced vision about the ups and downs of life, so they're depressing. A writer can create a terrible character who does cruel and terrifying deeds, but if there is some sense of humor in the character, the reader is intrigued enough to stay with the character. That doesn't mean that he admires the character, just that he is fascinated. And hopeful. Humor suggests that a character has a seed of redemption in him, the possibility that he could be a better person. Alex in Anthony Burgess's *A Clockwork Orange* is a murderer, but his sense of humor and love of Beethoven give the reader some hope that he will change. (See "Satire" later for more on this work.) However, this hope usually only pertains to the main characters. Minor characters may be evil and funny without any hope of redemption, for example, Christopher Walken's character in *True Romance* is an evil mobster who will never change, but he's still amusing.

At this point, we should distinguish between *comic fiction* and *comic scenes*:

  ❀ **Comic fiction** would suggest that the entire story features humor as its dominant tone even if the events ultimately prove tragic, such as the film *Dr. Strangelove*, which ends with the implied destruction of the world. We'll discuss this more later under satire.

🌢 **Comic scenes** are merely individual scenes that are meant to amuse, whether as a respite from emotional intensity or plot suspense. These are deliberate moments of humor. If the entire story is mostly comic scenes, you have comic fiction.

In general, the techniques of getting a laugh are the same in both categories. What you'll have to decide is how much humor you want and where you want to place it to achieve whatever effect you're looking for.

The World According to Comic Fiction

Comedy is tragedy turned on its head—or better yet, with a pie in the face. The first Greek dramas were tragedies; comedies appeared about fifty years later as exaggerations of the tragedies. Here's what I mean: Plant a bomb in a school and that's drama, possibly tragedy. Plant a bomb in a school and have a group of inept nerdy students find the bomb and toss it back and forth like a hot potato, nearly dropping it, and that's comedy. Yes, it's still a bomb and lives are still at risk. But in the drama, we don't know whether lives will be lost; in the comedy, we're certain they won't be or, if they are, it will be handled in such an exaggerated way that it is funny (as in dark comedies such as the film *Heathers*).

Comic fiction has three basic genres: *goofball*, *satire* and *romantic comedy*. Goofball exists to make the audience laugh, nothing more. Romantic comedy and satire, however, each have a specific formula and use the formula to make a larger statement about the world, what is known as its *world vision*. Most writers are intuitively familiar with these formulas, the result of reading and watching thousands of stories. Beginning writers imitate the patterns, but often clumsily because they don't understand why the pattern exists. We're going to change that right now.

GOOFBALL

This is the simplest form—the amoeba of comedy writing. Basically, it's a grab bag of every kind of humor device there is.

The goal is simply to have a string of funny scenes. There is no particular world vision, no social commentary, no insight to human nature. Just absurdity followed by even more absurdity. The *Airplane* and *Naked Gun* series are examples of this genre. Sometimes these are the funniest stories precisely because there are no real stakes and the audience feels free to let themselves go. *Dumb & Dumber* and *Ace Ventura: Pet Detective* masquerade as romantic comedies, but at heart are goofball comedies.

SATIRE

There is a difference between satiric and satire. Satiric describes a specific scene or moment in a story; satire describes the entire work. Satiric refers to skits on *Saturday Night Live* and *Mad TV*; satire refers to the world vision of such works as *Gulliver's Travels* and *Catch-22*. Both have the same goal: to change people's behavior. Both use the same technique to achieve this goal: exaggeration. But while the satiric focuses on a moment of amusement and insight, satire looks at the bigger picture. As a result, satire is often a much darker vision than any other genre. It works like this:

- Start the story with wildly amusing, over-the-top exaggerations in characterization and/or plot. In the beginning of Jonathan Swift's *Gulliver's Travels*, Gulliver is a doctor who is shipwrecked in a land where he is a giant and everyone else is tiny. When the palace catches on fire, Gulliver urinates on the fire, extinguishing the flames. Of course, the Lilliputians debate whether to honor him as a hero or execute him for desecrating the palace. In the opening of Bruce Jay Friedman's play, *Steambath*, the protagonist Tandy can't figure out how he wound up naked in a steambath with some Puerto Rican janitor who everyone says is God. The humor in the first part of a satire is edgy, but generally conventional. Just laughs.

- Next, shift the tone of the humor so it becomes darker. Where before the stakes seemed distant or involved slapstick physical danger, now the danger is more real. The stakes are often not just about physical death, but the pain and suffering we endure while alive. Gulliver goes to another land in which he experiences the most savage aspect of human beings in the form of Yahoos, who viciously slaughter the kindly, more "humane" species, the horses who befriend him. Tandy, too, experiences the horror of realizing that all that he stood for as a human was shallow and self-serving, giving him no joy.

✿ Finally, end the story with the total devastation of the protagonist. Gulliver, having returned to England with all his naive notions of hope about humanity, immortality and sex destroyed, refuses to leave his home because everyone outside reminds him of the Yahoos. Tandy, after seeming to convince God to let him return to his life, comes to accept that he'd wasted his life by always living for the future, never enjoying the moment as it was happening. In the end, he doesn't even want to go back.

The reason for this bleak spiral is to shock the audience into changing the way they behave. Satire is a cautionary vision. It projects the way the world might become—or you might become—unless you wise up and change yourself and/or the world. In this way, satire is very much like a morality story on the same level as *The Boy Who Cried Wolf* and other children's tales in which bad behavior results in the death of the child.

Considering the grim finale, what's funny about such stories? As I said, exaggeration. No one will forget the image of actor Slim Pickens bronco-riding the atom bomb out of the plane as it drops on Moscow. In the film *The President's Analyst*, the mystery conspirators trying to take over the world turn out to be the phone company.

ROMANTIC COMEDY

This is an ancient formula: boy meets girl, boy loses girl, boy gets girl. Seems simple enough, but it's a little more complicated.

Boy Meets Girl. The lovers meet and fall passionately in love.

Boy Loses Girl. There's no story if the lovers don't split. This is the conflict of the story, creating the suspense. However, the suspense isn't really around the question of whether or not they'll get together; it's how. There are two things that cause the lovers to split up: (1) Egos. When a couple comes together, each must give up some aspect of his or her self in order to form a "couple." It's difficult for selfish individuals to understand that the whole (couple) can be greater than the sum of its parts (lovers). (2) A corrupt official or relative who tries to keep the lovers apart. This character represents the kind of person who never overcame his ego, a person unable to be selfless. In that way, the character is a warning of the kind of person each lover might become if they don't wise up. (By the end of the story, the character is either defeated or won over to the lovers' side.)

Boy Gets Girl. The lovers overcome their egos and the corrupt official to become a couple again. However, the thing that brings them back together is not just a sudden desire or maturity, it's a device known as *deus ex machina* (machinery of the gods). Originally in Greek drama this meant that a god was literally lowered or raised up onto the stage for the purpose of righting the injustices. In modern storytelling, the *deus ex machina* manifests itself as an unexpected coincidence, something "accidental" that allows the lovers to realize how they really feel and then act upon it. Look at every romantic comedy and you'll find this device. Although it may seem like an artificial contrivance, it is the very heart of this genre. It represents the theme that the world is basically a good place and there is some sort of Intelligence or Force or God who cares about what happens here. If one has faith in this universal order, then all things will work out—with its help. And so the lovers are brought together through the coincidence created by the unseen hand. In the end, the lovers come together in marriage—or symbolic marriage. The marriage symbolizes the ability of individuals to overcome their selfishness to form a selfless relationship. And if these two individuals can do it, so can the world in order to form a perfect community, as is the desire of the Universal Intelligence.

This is the basic plot of most romantic comedies as well as romance novels. *His Girl Friday*, *Pretty Woman* and *You've Got Mail* follow this pattern, as do musical comedies such as *My Fair Lady* and *Oklahoma!* There are some variations. *My Best Friend's Wedding* is the same story, but told from the corrupt relative's point of view. Julia Roberts's character tries to get in the way of the lovers. A *deus ex machina* (a phony e-mail that accidentally gets sent) intervenes, which sets into motion a series of events to bring the lovers back together. The play *The Fantastiks* satirizes the formula as well as the notion of romantic love, but in the end gives way to sentimentality by bringing the lovers back together.

Squeeze the Moment

One of the main faults with beginning writers trying to write comedy is that they try to translate film comedy to written-page comedy, and that doesn't always work. There's a big difference between visual and written comedy. Slapstick can work on the page, but its success depends not just on describing the action, but describing it in an amusing way. Word choice and style sell the humor. Another warning: Don't tell jokes, especially old ones or ones you got off the Internet. If you've heard it, chances are so has the reader.

The two major categories of humor in a scene are *situational* and *verbal*. Situational depends upon the physical situation that the characters are in, which is the same concept as the television sitcom (situational comedy). Throw a bigoted blue collar worker, mousy wife, sexy daughter and loud-mouthed liberal son-in-law together and you have *All in the Family*. As if that wasn't enough of a situation to spark comedy, each episode created a situation that forced the members of the household to confront each other (e.g., black neighbors move in). The situation in *Friends* is even simpler: six emotionally insecure friends—three female, three male—confront romantic and career crises. Much of the conflict of this situation is caused by sexual tension and their extreme personality quirks (e.g., Monica's obsession with order and cleanliness).

SITUATIONAL COMEDY

The key to *situational comedy* is that it forces conflict and confrontation, the very same ingredients to drama. But while drama explores the serious issues that arise from such a situation, comedy makes fun of the situation. Here's an example from my first novel, *The Goulden Fleece*, which I wrote when I was twenty (hence the emphasis on physical humor). Protagonist Harry Gould is a small-time grifter who owes money to just about everyone in New York City. In fact, when two collection hoods, Gus and J.J., start working him over in the first chapter, he can't even be sure which loan shark they work for. This is the ending of the scene after J.J. skins his knuckles on Harry's teeth while punching him in the mouth.

"Christ!" he cried, shaking his hand, "The son of a bitch bit my goddamn hand." He appraised the damage as best he could in the dark alley. Then, having made his diagnosis, he began to tenderly suck the wound.

"How bad is it, J.J.?" Gus asked.

J.J. practiced opening and closing his hand. "Let me try again."

Gus tightened his grip on my arms as J.J. punched me in the stomach, quickly stepping back to protect his shoes from me retching on them again. He blew on his hand and sucked on the wound again. "It's no use. It hurts too much." Then he glared at me accusingly. "Christ, I hope I didn't catch no disease from him. I guess you'll have to take over while I hold him."

Gus hesitated, not so much holding me back as holding me up.

"To tell the truth, J.J., I'm not much in the mood tonight."

"What do you mean you're not in the mood?"

Gus shrugged, lowered his eyes.

"What's the matter, pal?" J.J. asked compassionately.

"I don't know. I think it's my ulcer acting up again. I shouldn't have had that second helping of ravioli tonight. You know how spicy they make it at Mama Leone's. Ever since I've had a lot of gas and acid." He released me with one hand to rub his stomach and belch as an offer of proof. He quickly snagged me as I began to sag to the ground.

"I told you so!" J.J. said in an I-told-you-so voice. "I told you that's what would happen, but you just wouldn't listen. How many glasses of milk have you had today?"

"One," Gus answered sheepishly.

"That's what I thought!" And you know you're supposed to have at least three. Minimum. Now what are we going to do with this guy?"

If this were played realistically, it would be painfully dramatic: A man is beaten senseless by two thugs. But I shift the focus from realism to slapstick. First, I don't describe the blood flying from Harry's nose and mouth. That would disturb the reader so he wouldn't be able to enjoy the humor. Second, the thugs discuss their dedication to their careers instead of making brutal threats.

Sometimes situational comedy is actually dark comedy with terrible things happening, but being done in such an exaggerated way as to elicit both the darkness and the humor of the situation. This is similar to satire except that it seeks to reveal an insight into a situation in order for us to experience a degree of compassion rather than frighten us into changing our behavior. In Stephen Dixon's short story, "The Signing," the narrator's wife dies in the first sentence. He staggers off in a grief-induced daze. A security guard follows him, trying to get him to sign a document releasing her body parts for transplant. Too devastated to respond, he climbs on a bus with the security guard sitting beside him. In order to ease his pain, the narrator suddenly decides to get rid of everything his wife touched.

> *"Do what you want with her body. There's nothing I ever want to have to do with her again. I'll never speak her name. Never go back to her apartment. Our car I'm going to let rot in the street till it's towed away. This wristwatch. She bought it for me and wore it a few times herself." I throw it out the window.*
>
> *"Why didn't you just pass it on back here?" the man behind me says.*

Notice the long monologue of grief followed by the short punch line. The punch line gets its power from both the length and intensity of the emotional speech. The humor works because the line is unexpected—a practical response in the face of the illogic of grief.

A similar technique is used to open David Ordan's short story, "Any Minute Mom Should Come Blasting Through the Door":

> *Mom died in the middle of making me a sandwich. If I had*
> *known it was going to kill her, I never would have asked.*

This story is about grief and how the death of his mother destroys the relationship between the narrator and his father. But the tone, while dark and serious, also has those moments of levity that make the reader care more about the character and trust his version of what happened because the humor appears to give him a balanced view. Also, it creates a sense of loss. Since the story is more humorous at the beginning than at the end, the reader sees in a tangible way that some bright part of the narrator has been dimmed.

VERBAL COMEDY

Verbal comedy is often the spice that makes the situations funny. It involves mostly internal monologues, descriptions or dialogue.

Internal monologue. This is usually the first-person narrator revealing his thoughts, philosophies, hopes and fears through his observations of the world at large. In Nick Hornby's *High Fidelity*, he describes the obsession of himself and his friends when they were young boys with trying to touch girls' breasts:

> *...It was as if breasts were little pieces of property that had been*
> *unlawfully annexed by the opposite sex—they were rightfully*
> *ours and we wanted them back.*

Later in the same novel, he discusses the issue of foreplay:

> *Read any woman's magazine and you'll see the same com-*
> *plaint over and over again: men—those little boys ten or twen-*
> *ty or thirty years on—are hopeless in bed. They are not*
> *interested in "foreplay"; they have no desire to stimulate the*
> *erogenous zones of the opposite sex; they are selfish, greedy,*
> *clumsy, unsophisticated. These complaints, you can't help feel-*
> *ing, are kind of ironic. Back then, all we wanted was foreplay,*
> *and girls weren't interested. They didn't want to be touched, ca-*
> *ressed, stimulated, aroused; in fact, they used to thump us if we*
> *tried. It's not surprising then, that we're not very good at all*
> *that. We spent two or three long and extremely formative years*

> *being told very forcibly not to even think about it. Between the*
> *ages of fourteen and twenty-four, foreplay changes from being*
> *something that boys want to do and girls don't, to something*
> *that women want and men can't be bothered with.... The per-*
> *fect match, if you ask me, is between the* Cosmo *woman and*
> *the fourteen-year-old boy.*

This particular passage is crucial because the novel is about a
man trying to figure out why his relationships with women
have always gone bad. That setup gives him an opportunity to
philosophize about the sexes in general. This form of internal
monologue can be funny, not only because of what it reveals
about the character but because of the insight of the social
commentary.

It's the situation that provides the opportunity for the internal monologue. Sometimes the situation may be absurd,
but the monologue is all the more poignant because of the contrast. Sometimes the absurdity of the situation tells us more
about the character than what he tells us in his internal monologue (see "Unreliable Narrator" in chapter four). In Leonard
Michaels's short story, "City Boy," the narrator Phillip is caught
having sex in the living room of his girlfriend's home—caught
by the father. Phillip panics and rushes out of the apartment
completely naked. He tries to decide what to do:

> *I needed poise. Without poise the street was impossible. Blood*
> *shot to my brain, thought blossomed. I'd walk on my hands.*
> *Beards were fashionable. I kicked up my feet, kicked the eleva-*
> *tor button, faced the door and waited.*

Here the narrator decides that the only way he can go out onto
the streets of New York City naked is if he walks on his hands
because then people won't notice he's naked; they'll think he
has a beard. Yes, it's absurd; that's the point. The story is about
a character who believes he's in complete control of his life, but
all along the reader sees him making absurd decisions that
prove the opposite.

Description. This focuses on an amusing description of
people, actions or setting. Both of the following focus on fe-

male narrators describing their own breasts. While both descriptions are comic, each tries to achieve a different effect. The first passage is in Jen Banbury's novel, *Like a Hole in the Head*, immediately after the narrator has bicycled to work.

> *Eleven o'clock and it was already hot as hell. By the time I got to the bookstore I could feel the sweat rolling down my cleavage. Like a ride at a water park. The Boob Slide. Little kids screaming the whole way down.*

This passage is early in the Laramie Dunaway novel, *Lessons in Survival*. She's reluctantly trying to get ready for a blind date.

> *I struggled to get up off the bed, but the best I could muster was to raise my head a couple inches. From this angle, I could look down my own blouse and see my 34B breasts shifting abruptly as if they were scoops of ice cream melting out from under the upended cones of my bra cups. I plucked my blouse up into a tent so I could look down and measure what damage age and gravity had done to me. Each breast reminded me of the oversized gelatinous head of an octopus. Maybe breast implants weren't such a bad idea. Some of the women at school had them and seemed happy. Mitzi had them (and how). I nudged my left breast with my fingertip, like poking a corpse's cheek. My boobs sagged in a way that reminded me too much of my sagging life in general. The way people start to resemble their dogs after a while. Perhaps perkier breasts would make my whole life perkier. Breasts that can stand up to the onslaught of life reflect an owner who can do likewise. Bulletproof boobs. Tits with a mission. I grabbed both of my flannel-covered breasts, one in each hand, and said aloud, "Shape up, guys. It's a big world and you've got your whole life ahead of you. You've come in here boobs, but you're leaving here knockers."*
>
> *I started to laugh, but when I looked over at the doorway, I saw Mitzi standing there. Next to her was a handsome young uniformed cop. They stared at me.*
>
> *Mitzi applauded. "Is this your new ventriloquist act? I love your dummies." She laughed. "Blue, meet your blind date*

Dave. Dave is a god among men. Dave, isn't she everything I said she was? Shy, demure, conservative."

The first example tells the reader what kind of person the narrator is through the kind of humor she prefers: self-deprecatory, witty, offbeat. The second example is meant to convey the same humorous characteristics about the narrator, Blue. However, I also wanted to convey the deeper anxiety and desperation that she was feeling. Her dissatisfaction with her breasts reflected her dissatisfaction with her life. I had her focus on her breasts to show the emotion because breasts symbolize how women are forced to live under the tyranny of ideals of physical perfection that cannot be met. No wonder she feels intimidated and betrayed by the imaginary imperfections of her own body. However, I didn't want the scene to spiral into self-pity, so I immediately undercut the serious emotion through situational comedy: She's talking to her breasts when her blind date walks in. The embarrassment the reader knows she must feel is funny. Add to that the wisecrack from her roommate Mitzi and the tone has shifted from descriptive comedy, which is slightly slower in pace, to situational comedy, which picks up the pace because it focuses on plot development.

One of the major forms of descriptive verbal comedy is the use of clever *similes*, comparing two seemingly dissimilar things to show their similarities. These are the punch lines of fiction writers. The advantage is that, when done with wit and grace, they add a rich dimension to the style and story. The disadvantage is that when the similes are strained, forced or too frequent, they completely destroy the reader's ability to immerse herself in the story. The good simile enhances the story; the bad one calls attention to itself and distracts the reader. Here are a couple of good examples:

He jerked at the sound of my voice, like a dog caught drinking from the toilet bowl.
> Jen Banbury's *Like a Hole in the Head*

I'd stopped shaving my armpits. Legs, too, though my hair there was too blond and fine to be noticeable. But the un-

> *derarm hair came in mysteriously dark and thick, like exotic underbrush from the Brazilian rain forest, the extract of which might cure cancer.*
>
> Laramie Dunaway's *Lessons in Survival*

Descriptive verbal comedy relies on unexpected word choices that elevate the action or object being described. In the following passage from Stanley Elkin's short story, "A Poetics for Bullies," the narrator, Push the Bully, describes his artistry in picking on certain kids.

> *A kid is going downtown on the elevated train. He's got his little suit on, his shoes are shined, he wears a cap. This is a kid going to the travel bureaus, the foreign tourist offices to get brochures, maps, pictures of the mountains for a unit at his school—a kid looking for extra credit. I follow him. He comes out of the Italian Tourist Information Center. His arms are full. I move from my place at the window. I follow for two blocks and bump into him as he steps from the curb. It's a collision—the pamphlets fall from his arms. Pretending confusion, I walk on his paper Florence. I grind my heel in his Riviera. I climb Vesuvius and sack his Rome and dance on the Isle of Capri.*

The last three sentences are funny because his word choices create imagery that is much more expressive than just a boy stepping on a paper map. Because it's in Push's point of view, the word choices reveal an intelligence that suggests his actions are motivated by more than the desire to bully. Plus, because it's a funny scene, we care more about discovering what those motivations are.

Just as there are different shades of red, there are different intensity levels of humor. It's important to select the intensity level suitable for the tone of the scene. Sometimes the humor is more of a tint than an actual color, just enough to establish the narrator's point of view. Irony and sarcasm are also part of the humor spectrum, but you have to be careful not to overuse them. Irony and sarcasm can quickly become intrusive and self-congratulatory, alienating the reader. However, in the hands of a subtle writer like Lorrie Moore, it's compelling. In this passage from her short story, "You're Ugly, Too," Moore is describing the protagonist's students:

> *Her students were by and large good Midwesterners, spacey with estrogen from large quantities of meat and cheese. They shared their parents' suburban values; their parents had given them things, things, things. They were complacent. They had been purchased. They were armed with a healthy vagueness about anything historical or geographic. They seemed actually to know very little about anything, but they were extremely good-natured about it, "All those states in the east are so tiny and jagged and bunched up," complained one of her undergraduates....*

With Moore, it's the word choices that jump out: "spacey with estrogen" and "armed with a healthy vagueness." This is fresh and original language that makes reading the passage exciting. Notice, too, how once Moore comments on how little they know, she follows it up with a line of dialogue as an example. That's the punch line. This is not laugh-aloud humor; it's more of a nodding-in-appreciation humor.

Dialogue. This is the witty banter of characters. Of course, one person's wit is another's mindless chatter. Some find Oscar Wilde's plays delightfully urbane; others want to run screaming into Blockbuster to rent the latest Adam Sandler for some *real* wit. Again, you'll have to figure out for yourself what your definition of witty banter is. The following example comes from Leonard Michaels's "City Boy" again. Phillip, still naked but walking on his legs now, goes into the subway to go home. Being naked, he has no money. He asks the African-American man in the change booth to let him go through for free.

> *He merely looked at me. Then his eyes flashed like fangs. Instinctively, I guessed what he felt. He didn't owe favors to a white man. He didn't have to bring his allegiance to the transit authority into question for my sake.*
> *"Hey, man, you're naked?"*
> *"Yes."*
> *"Step back a little."*
> *I stepped back. "You're naked."*

> *I nodded.*
> *"Get your naked ass the hell out of here."*
> *"Sir," I said, "I know these are difficult times, but can't we be reasonable? I know that..."*
> *"Scat, mother, go home."*

The humor here is a combination of the dialogue and the narrative, neither one working without the other.

1. The line about the "allegiance to the transit authority" is funny phrasing. If Michaels had said, "He didn't want to risk his job with the transit authority for my sake," he'd have said the exact same thing, but it wouldn't have been funny. Why? Because who in his right mind actually has *allegiance* to the transit authority? One might have duty or responsibility, but the word allegiance is so over the top, it's funny.

2. The dialogue exchange up to the last two lines is basically the written version of a double take (swiveling the head twice in reaction) or a spit take (reacting while drinking by involuntarily spitting the liquid). It's funny because the narrator is so nonchalant about his situation while the tollbooth man can't get over what he's seeing.

3. The line that begins with "Sir" is funny because Phillip tries to talk his way out of his predicament by appealing to the larger social issue of "these are difficult times" (referring to the tension between the races). This is what Phillip constantly does throughout the story; he elevates his self-created minor problems to universal issues. Because this is a pattern, it gets funnier each time.

Final Word

Writing comic fiction scenes is the most difficult of all writing because it requires endless tinkering with lines and word choices to get the maximum comedy mileage. And, unlike stage or screen, you can't rely on the impact of instant visuals. You have to conjure them secondhand through description. Yes, there are many techniques involved, but the essence of comedy writing is understanding the connection between contrasts. It's funny when someone trips and falls because it catches us by surprise, but it's funnier if the person falling is dressed formally rather than in overalls. The "hair gel" scene in *There's Something About Mary* is funny because it takes us by surprise, but is even funnier because of the contrast of beautiful Cameron Diaz doing it as opposed to a less attractive actress. First, look for the surprise. Second, play with ways to exaggerate the contrast between the action and the people it's happening to.

The people who are funniest in person do not necessarily make the funniest writers. Just because you don't get laughs at parties by jamming breadsticks up your nose doesn't mean you can't write comic scenes. I've written a dozen or so comic novels and a few comedy film scripts. My wife is the funniest writer and person that I've ever met. We're both very shy. When we go to parties, we tend to stand off by ourselves and crack each other up. A lot of my students who write hilarious comedy are the same way—quiet, shy, self-contained—which means you shouldn't be intimidated by how you imagine funny people are supposed to be. You have an idea for something funny? Write it. If it makes you laugh, there's a good chance others will laugh, too.

TIP

Comedy and Publishing

A practical note here: Every once in a while a humorous novel like Helen Fielding's Bridget Jones' Diary *or Nick Hornby's* High Fidelity *will hit the best-seller lists, but in general, humor in fiction is underappreciated and, in some genres, openly discouraged. The mystery and suspense genres are especially resistant to humor. Editors have consistently stated that humorous mysteries are hard to sell. It's the same with suspense, science fiction, Westerns and even mainstream. Part of the reason is what we discussed at the beginning of this chapter: taste. It's easier to make a large group of people cry than laugh. There seems to be a general agreement about what is sad, but humor is more of a niche and it will be harder to sell your novel to a large group. I don't say this to discourage you from writing a humorous novel—there are plenty of successes to serve as examples. Just be aware that it's a harder sell.*

❧ 11 ❧
LOVE & LUST:
ROMANTIC & SEX SCENES

"Since we no longer write about the union with God, writing about sex has become the ultimate test for the writer; to communicate the incommunicable."

Michele Roberts

"Reading about sex in yesterday's novels is like watching people smoke in old films."

Fay Weldon

"Literature is mostly about having sex and not much about having children. Life is the other way round."

David Lodge

❧ PLEASE NOTE: If you're offended by explicit discussions of sex and body parts, you may want to skip this chapter.

Sex is a crucial part of the human experience. This is attested to by the fact that the majority of most societies' moral teachings are built around sexual issues. How a person views, approaches, pursues and conducts sex reveals a lot about who she is. It's such a litmus test of character because it reveals how a person deals with and expresses her most primal passion. In fact, many people define themselves through their sexuality: Being attractive to others and having fulfilling sex makes a person feel confident; the loss of sexual appetite or desirability can lead to severe depression. Certainly the fact that most advertisements use sex—usually the promise of it—to sell products tells you how important it is in our society. It follows that if sex is so important in our society, it's probably going to play a big role in our literature. And so it does.

There are two basic components of sex and, therefore, of sex scenes: the *pursuit* and the *culmination*. The pursuit is the *romantic* aspect: when two people do the courting dance, enraptured with the mere sight and touch of each other. The culmination is the *sexual* act: when the two lovers finally reveal to each other not only their naked bodies, but also their bare souls. Sometimes the romance and sex happen in the same scene, sometimes in separate scenes. Some writers emphasize romance over sex, some emphasize sex over romance, some balance the two. However they are combined, each has various approaches and techniques to achieve specific effects. Learning those methods will help you determine what your story needs. A good way to distinguish between romance and sex is in terms of writing a story. When a writer first gets an idea for a story, he's excited about the possibilities, constantly dotes on every aspect of the story and is convinced this will be the best work he's ever written. That's romance. The actual writing of the story is like sex: It involves a physical act that requires technique. It is always different than you imagined it would be— not necessarily better or worse, just different. And it can be emotionally and physically exhausting.

Love Me Tender, Love Me True

Romantic scenes are primarily about love. Sure, sex is a part of the equation, but it is not the focus. Rather, sex is treated as a symbolic act, a by-product of romance in the way that the honeymoon is a by-product of the much more important event of the wedding. Unlike the relationship between suspense and action scenes, romantic scenes are not promise scenes with sex as the payoff. Romantic scenes are in themselves the payoff. If written correctly, the reader will be fully satisfied with where the relationship is at that end of the scene, regardless of whether or not sex has been a part of it.

Romantic scenes create a mood in which the reader cares about nothing else at that moment than whether or not the lovers will get together or remain together. This is accomplished by establishing *emotional stakes*. Early in the story, the writer must emphasize how important a romantic relationship is to the protagonist, even if the protagonist is not aware of its importance. There are lots of ways to show this:

1. The protagonist is just out of a relationship and is feeling isolated.
2. The lovers already know each other and are just starting a relationship.
3. The lovers haven't met yet. Part of the suspense is knowing that they will meet, which the reader anxiously anticipates.

On a very basic level, every story is about how characters confront conflict and either change for the better (happy ending) or don't change at all or change for the worse (sad ending). In general, what makes the impending romantic relationship so important is that it provides the means by which the protagonist(s) may achieve change for the good: some sense of redemption, salvation or completion. I don't want those words to be too loaded, but each expresses a different aspect of the character's need, which is often what the whole story is about.

In other words, romance is about hope.

Since we have the ability to love—to put someone else's needs above our own—we have the potential to change for the better (see also "Romantic Comedy" in chapter eleven). Let's look at how each of those terms works.

REDEMPTION

Setup: The protagonist has a history of bad relationships, either numerous or one really devastating one. This has left him with an inability to give himself over to love. He interacts with people in a polite but reserved manner. He may have numerous sexual affairs, but none that he has any passion for.

Payoff: For him to be redeemed, he must fall in love, despite his initial resistance. Love sets him free from the emotional straitjacket and allows him to embrace not only his lover, but the larger community as well.

SALVATION

Setup: The protagonist is to some extent antisocial. He may be a thief, liar or womanizer—or worse. His inability to love doesn't come from bad love experiences, but rather because he's never been *able* to love. The reader can see his ways are leading him to self-destruction, but he can't. He is so self-obsessed that when he meets someone who might change his ways, he threatens to push her away for good.

Payoff: As with the redemption approach, love provides the opportunity for him to see the world on a larger, richer scale than he's experienced before. By embracing his lover, he embraces a whole new life and lifestyle.

COMPLETION

Setup: This is a straightforward romance with both characters looking for love but unsure of how to recognize it, express it or accept it. There could be elements of either or both of the above categories in this, but the main focus is that the lovers recognize they do not feel complete without someone to love and be loved by.

Payoff: The lovers find each other, overcome external and internal obstacles and remain together.

The payoff in each of these categories is what we hope for—it creates the stakes. However, the story doesn't have to turn out happily. Characters can be unable to overcome their emotional barriers and end up alone. If that happens, then the payoff isn't what happens to the characters; *it's what happens to the readers.* The readers are moved and given some insight about the nature of and importance of relationships, and warned about what can go wrong and the devastating effects of losing love.

How do you create romance in a scene? Pretty much the same way you do in real life. You bring the lovers together, then make the reader care about whether or not they remain together. The specifics of what happens in such a scene is where the creativity and depth of the individual writer comes in. A lesser writer would set such a scene in the predictable place: a candlelit bedroom with romantic music in the background. The lovers would gaze longingly into each other's eyes and discuss, in hushed tones, how each fulfills the other. Seen it a billion times. But play with the concept a little and you have a more interesting, and maybe even more meaningful, romantic scene. One popular variation of this "confessional" scene is to have the male reveal in front of a crowd how he feels about the female. In *Dirty Dancing*, Patrick Swayze tells the audience how Jennifer Grey made him a better man. In *Jerry Maguire*, Tom Cruise tells Renée Zellweger how much he loves her with a woman's support group watching. Dozens of films have someone testifying in a court case, only to reveal to the entire courtroom their love for someone else in the courtroom. This type of situational setup, which depends on the audience's reaction for part of its impact, tends to add a comical tone to the proceedings, so it's more a technique of the romantic comedy.

My preference is to have the characters alone somewhere, but not in a typically romantic setting. No candles, no fancy restaurants, no soft music. That smacks of contrivance, not only from the characters but from the author. It's so unimaginative that it makes the reader care less about the couple getting together. As for the dialogue, rather than the hushed tones, I prefer that the characters talk about different things until they finally discuss the relationship. And when they do discuss the relationship, it seems stronger if they're direct about it. If they speak too poetically, it again seems contrived and laughable. What's more romantic: a Hallmark card with fancy script sentiments printed inside or a handmade card with original drawings and poetry? The amount of effort and care that went into the handmade card is a direct reflection of the affection the creator has for the other person. The same with creating romantic scenes. When they seem stamped out of a romantic cookie cutter, they have less effect on the reader. Improvise.

Insert Tab A Into Slot B

It would be a big mistake for a writer to dismiss sex scenes as existing merely to titillate the reader. Yes, sometimes sex scenes exist for no other reason than they're a convention of the genre. Certain glitz novels and potboilers include them for the same reason many movies do: to attract the audience. But in the best of books, the sex scene is an integral part of the story, just as it is an integral part of our daily lives.

There are three kinds of sex scenes:

THE IMPLIED SEX SCENE

Description: This scene contains very little, if any, actual sexual contact. Characters may kiss, grope, grind, even start to undress. Then the scene ends. This is sometimes described as the *closed door sex scene* because in old movies, just as things began to heat up, the bedroom door would close and we were left to imagine what happened behind the door.

Advantages: Some genres, such as some categories of romance, don't permit explicit sexual descriptions. In some cases, having the reader witness the sex, even if modestly described, can change the tone of the story by focusing on the passion rather than on the spiritual connection. Or the writer may not feel comfortable with anything more than implying sex.

Disadvantages: It can make the story seem less realistic and the characters more superficial. Love is usually a combination of hot passion and spiritual connection; emphasizing one over the other can make the story seem simplistic.

THE MODEST SEX SCENE

Description: In this version, there is sexual contact, probably even intercourse or oral sex, but the details are murky and the brief descriptive lines are poetic. This is used when the writer wants to avoid the naked passion of the act to imply a spiritual bonding.

Advantages: The reader still experiences the passion of the couple, so she has some idea what motivates their subsequent actions. The poetic word choices tell the reader that though the sex is a little more explicit, it's not the focus of the scene. Rather, it is the spice to the more important romantic aspect.

Disadvantages: Sometimes such a scene can seem contrived and unrealistic. While sex is sometimes a meaningful ascent to the heights of spiritual sharing, sometimes it's just sweaty passion, the crashing of two bodies desperate for connection. If overwritten, sex scenes can reduce the realism of the characters and the stakes.

THE EXPLICIT SEX SCENE

Description: The descriptions of the sex are very detailed and explicit. Also, the sex may be varied, including unusual locations, situations and/or acts.

Advantages: The reader is meant to feel the intensity of the couple's passion even to the point of being aroused. Sure, it could be simply for prurient reasons, but not necessarily. Intense passion can be a hugely motivating force, causing people to change their lives or do uncharacteristic things. For example, a forty-five-year-old man with two children, a loving wife and a good job suddenly abandons all of them to live in a crappy apartment with a nineteen-year-old struggling actress. The first inclination of the reader is to dismiss this person as going through the clichéd midlife crisis, but that's because it's a comfortable explanation of a chaotic situation. If the writer wants the reader to go beyond the smug conclusions, she must make the reader experience the same passion as that man. This is one instance when a highly charged erotic scene is called for. In the most recent film version of James Cain's novel, *The Postman Always Rings Twice*, the lovers plot to kill the woman's husband. The raw sex scene between Jack Nicholson and Jessica Lange is meant to make the audience experience the passion that drives them beyond conventional morality to murder.

Disadvantages: The line between literary eroticism and cheesy smut is difficult to walk. Some readers will think that any explicit sex is smut, but if you think it is called for, you can't be intimidated by that notion. Those are not your target readers anyway, so you must go with what the story demands. Also, it's difficult to write literary erotica because there are only so many ways you can describe the physical act of sex. Often beginning writers will overdo the metaphors and the scene can become unintentionally comic.

Your sex scenes will most likely fall into one of the above categories. First, decide what you hope the sex scene will accomplish: What will it reveal about the characters in order to compel them to do whatever the plot calls for them to do, and make the reader care about them more and understand their actions better?

Following is an example of the implied sex scene from Elmore Leonard's *Be Cool*, the sequel to *Get Shorty*. In this scene, Chili Palmer is about to have sex for the first time with a powerful Hollywood studio executive.

She said, "I'm dying for us to kiss."

Serious about it but still girlish. Her eyes, her mouth right there, clean, not wearing lipstick.

He said, "I was thinking the same thing, Elaine," and slipped his hands around her slim body to bring them together, saw her eyes close and they kissed, got the right fit, and then both were into it all the way until they came apart and looked at each other, both smiling a little, relieved there was no problem with breath or being too intense or sloppy. No, it was great.

Elaine said, "We could fool around a little, see where it takes us."

Chili said, "We fool around lying down we're there."

Elaine said, "Let's go take our clothes off," and led him upstairs.

This is the last part of the scene, the part that leads to the sex, at which point the door is closed—kind of, which I'll get to in a minute. For now, what I want you to notice is the technique, the choices Leonard made and why. This scene isn't about the sex; it's about two people coming together for the first time, recognizing they both have a desire for each other and figuring out how to act on it. The romance is straightforward; no purple prose or overblown declarations of love. These are two adults who've both been around a bit, know what they want and aren't shy about pursuing it. Yet it's also subtly demure, each feeling the other out, not making a move. They use dialogue, which presents their intelligence, to seduce each other. Even the dialogue is low-key. Notice that the dialogue begins with the speaker's name followed by "said." With a lesser writer, this repetition might seem boring, but Leonard wants to undercut the sexual tension by downplaying the action and focusing only on the dialogue. The bareness of the qualifiers ("Elaine said") emphasizes their dialogue.

This next section is the entire scene that follows the one above.

They made love and it went well.

They rested and made love again and it went even better, way better.

> *In the dark, arms around each other, he asked her if she was Jewish. She said yeah, all her life. He said he wondered because she kept saying Jesus a lot while they were doing it. She asked him what he was and he said mostly Italian. He asked her how old she was. She said forty-four. He said he was surprised she didn't duck the question, didn't even hesitate. She asked him why, what was wrong with being forty-four? Right after that she said she was thinking about having a cigarette. He said he thought she'd quit. She said she decided it would be okay on special occasions. Did he mind? He said no, not at all, he'd have a smoke too. He said unless she wanted to go for it again. She said they'd better not press their luck. Were his ears still ringing? He said just a little.*

This scene is the important part of the romance because it's about the conversation after sex, how they get to know each other. They don't talk about anything important, nothing crucial to the plot that's been going on for the previous 196 pages. It's the little stuff that adds up to a relationship. Notice that Leonard doesn't write this in dialogue format; rather, he summarizes what they're talking about, all in one paragraph. This makes it seem more intimate.

When Sex Isn't Just Sex

A sex scene isn't always about the sex. In fact, one can have a pretty explicit sex scene in which there is little sense of passion from the characters or arousal in the reader. This occurs when the sex scene is really about something else, usually about how the character is unfulfilled by what's going on, even though it's what she thinks she wants. Such a scene represents a character's conflict between what they think they want and what the reader recognizes they really need.

I wrote a few sex scenes into my novel *Lessons in Survival*. Their purpose was to show the development of the main character, Blue Erhardt, whose emotional development had been arrested ever since her parents were sent to prison for a bank robbery twenty years earlier. She had since spent her life proving that she was nothing like them, even to the point of marrying (and then divorcing) a cop.

In the first sex scene, Blue is having sex with her ex-husband, Lewis. He's a nice guy, but the reader already knows they don't belong together. She has sex with him only because her carefully created world is coming apart—her parents are about to be released from prison. She feels alone, afraid and vulnerable, and seeks Lewis's company.

The sex, however, is less than ideal for her. She spends the entire time thinking about the carpet they are lying upon, "a weary, mustard-colored shag that had endured how many renters, how many sweaty bodies depositing body oils and fluids into its ancient fibers." During Lewis's mediocre sexual performance, Blue starts to daydream about the dust mites in the carpet, which are feeding on the dead skin cells being rubbed from Blue's shoulders. Currently a biology teacher, this leads Blue to recall how her students reacted when she taught them about the mating practices of dust mites, which is not an arousing topic at all.

Blue goes back and forth between thinking about the dust mites and yawningly noticing what Lewis is doing with her body. She reaches orgasm, but even that isn't a big deal to her. When Lewis finally spends himself, he tries to show Blue a little tenderness; the sex has obviously been more meaningful to him than it has to her. The scene ends with this exchange:

> Lewis kissed my cheek and pulled me close. He smelled my hair and sighed. "This is nice," he said. "I could get used to this again."
>
> "Let's eat," I said.

This scene begins on page 44 of a 424-page book. It is Blue's first sex scene and obviously isn't about sex or passion; it's about loneliness, alienation and fear. Its function is to define Blue's re-

TIP
What to Call Sexual Parts

There are no set rules, but, in general, it's a good idea to use breasts, penis and vagina. Yes, it may sound a little clinical, but euphemisms like "alabaster honeydews," "throbbing member" and "love nest" just seem silly and make the sex scene seem more like slapstick. Avoid the words you'd tell your kids not to use: tits, cock and pussy, which sound like porn (unless you're writing porn). However, those same words could work if they are used in dialogue or in a specific character's point of view to reveal his or her attitude, upbringing or tone.

lationships to this point so the reader can see how far she has to go. The next scene introduces Russell "Rush" Poundstone, the character who will eventually become Blue's love interest, but because of this sex scene, I've established how hard it will be for him to overcome her emotional barriers. That creates stakes and makes the reader automatically root for the potential lover.

A hundred pages later, Blue and Rush get together for a romantic scene. Rush is a wannabe producer trying to sign Blue up for a Movie of the Week. In a previous scene, she had torn up his contract and thrown it in his face. In the following scene, she arrives at his motel room, scraped up and dirty after a mishap in the preceding chapter. This scene begins with Blue washing and shaving in Rush's bathroom, and goes to the end of the chapter. (*Note*: Rush makes fun of Blue's last name. He calls her Amelia because her last name is Erhardt, which she changed it to in honor of the pilot.)

> *I slipped out of my blouse and raised my arms. Puffball tufts of blonde hair with dark roots. Everything inside the body is dark when it first emerges. Hair. Urine. Feces. Blood. Babies. Five minutes later my armpits were nude again. Slick and pale as a halved pear.*
>
> *"Not that I care," Rush said through the door, "but if you've killed yourself I hope you did it in the tub. I hate mess."*
>
> *I rinsed Rush's razor and replaced it in the medicine cabinet.*
>
> *Then I put my blouse back on, feeling much better. Weightless again. No clone of my mother now, I didn't have to hide out any more in my cyst enclosures.*

The scene goes on with some light verbal sparring, and then we get to the clincher:

> *I quickly stepped into his arms. Actually, I pulled him into my arms. I kissed him on the mouth. Nothing sloppy, just some minor lip mashing. Junior high stuff. He was too surprised to participate much.*
>
> *He pushed me away. "What are you doing?" He patted*

his pocket. "Hey, where's my wallet?"

"Okay, I deserved that."

"Which? The insult or the kiss?"

"Where's your contract?"

"You tore it up, remember? That little lesson in psychology I'm still grateful for."

"You must have copies. You're the type."

He gave me a skeptical look. "What's going on, Blue?"

"You want me to sign or don't you?"

"Sure. I just want to know if this is going to be another opportunity for you to make a speech and give me third-degree paper cuts at the same time."

"Trust me, okay?"

"Trust?" He said the word as if he'd never heard it before. Then he shrugged. "Just give me a chance to put on my hockey mask before you throw it in my face, okay?" He went over to his briefcase and opened the lid. The little leather loops for pens each held a pen. The calculator pocket hugged a calculator. Very organized. "What made you change your mind? And what was that kiss all about?" He handed me a copy of the contract and a pen.

I signed it and gave both back.

"Do you have condoms?" I asked him. "Have you been tested for AIDS?"

"Well, it was more like a quiz really...."

I started for the door. "You want to play games, play with yourself."

He flopped onto the edge of the bed. "I'm not running after you, if that's what you're expecting. You've got some movie going on in your head here and you're writing it as you go along. Tell me the plot, who I'm supposed to be, I'll jump in."

I turned around and faced him, my voice crisp and businesslike as I could make it. "You want to have sex or not?"

"Have you been tested for AIDS?"

"Yes. I'm clean."

"Clean." He laughed at the word. Then his face got serious. "Why are you doing this, Amelia? A minute ago you wanted to eat my liver."

"I don't want to go into explanations, Poundcake. You

want to have sex or not? Not hypothetically, not sometime in the future. Right now. Right here. Actual fucking."

"Sure. Okay." He got up and grabbed Russell by the collar, ushering him into the bathroom. He closed the door and started pulling off his shirt.

I hesitated. I wasn't sure what I'd expected him to say or do. I wasn't even sure what I was going to do. I'd seen something in him a moment ago, seen the potential for trust. He was attractive, I'd felt that right from the beginning, but seeing him put his dog's toothbrush next to his own, it made me want to trust him. And why should I care if I sold my story to Hollywood? Rush had been right about that. Didn't I deserve a little something back for all the suffering I had gone through anyway?

I pulled off my blouse. The air-conditioned air stung my shaved armpits. I kept going, matching him clothing item for clothing item. Shoes. Pants. Underwear.

We stood naked on either side of the bed. The TV was still on, as if he figured I was going to back out at any second and he didn't want to miss the end of the show if I did.

"I'd read that you didn't shave your armpits," he said, nodding at my arms.

"You were misinformed."

He laughed. "Bogart. I should have figured you'd quote him about now. Who am I supposed to be, Lauren Bacall? You know how to whistle, don't ya?"

We stared at each other across the bed, daring the other to feel ashamed and either get dressed or jump under the covers. He put his hands on his hips and looked over my body. I went him one better, folding my arms behind my back. Nothing to hide here, pal.

His body was thin and almost hairless, except for a diamond-shaped patch over his sternum and a woolly circle around his penis. His arms were toned and his stomach lean, but there was a hint of a little growth around the middle, like the wax gathering at the bottom of a candle. His penis was semierect, not fully trusting of the situation.

He made a move toward the TV.

"Leave it on," I said. "I like the noise."

He shrugged, returned to his side of the bed, facing me.

"What's your plan?" he said. "We do it from across the bed without actually getting on it? You overestimate me, Amelia."

I pulled back the covers all the way, stripping them from the bed into a pile on the floor. This was going to be a lights-on, no-covers screw. I didn't want any soft music, dim lighting, snugly covers. Nothing romantic. Just biology.

I climbed on top of the sheet. He did the same.

"One thing," I said. "I'm not going down on you, okay?"

"Got it. And I'm not doing my animal calls, so don't even ask."

"I'm serious. If I've learned one thing about sex it's that if you swallow a man's come, he right away takes that as a validation of everything he believes in. Like you also have to swallow all his bullshit too." I was thinking about Dale. Until we'd had oral sex (I was the first to actually do it), he'd pretty much treated me as an equal. Once I'd swallowed his sperm, though, he assumed I agreed with him about everything and always looked surprised and hurt when I didn't. "This is just straight intercourse, okay?"

"Okay, no sucking. No swallowing. No eye gouging or hitting below the waist. Now go to your corners and come out screwing." He pushed a pillow against the headboard and leaned back on it. "Now, here are my rules. Maybe you're doing this because you're going through some kind of emotional turmoil. Maybe deep down you think that at the last second I'll get up and say I can't do this or some kind of gentlemanly bullshit like that. I won't. Not unless you tell me to. You say stop, I'll stop." He looked over at me, waiting.

I didn't say anything.

"Okay," he continued. "Maybe I'm taking advantage of the situation. No, I'm definitely taking advantage of the situation. You've had a huge emotional shock tonight. Tomorrow you'll probably regret this and be pissed at me. Thing is, I don't care. If you weren't trying to prove something right now, we'd probably never have sex. And I want to have sex with you, I really do. I just wish I was smart enough to figure out what it is you think this will prove."

"I'm not trying to prove anything. All you amateur analysts raised on TV psychology think you know so much. It's

> *kind of pathetic, really."*
>
> *He laughed. "Nothing gets me hotter than being called pathetic. Ooooh, baby!"*
>
> *I looked down at his penis which was even less stiff than before. "Is this going to be a problem for you?"*
>
> *"You referring to my being pathetic or my being limp?"*
>
> *"I didn't know men could use the word limp within a two-hour window of having sex. Some sort of superstition thing, like stepping on a sidewalk crack breaks your mother's back."*
>
> *He shrugged. "Maybe if we just shut up and see what happens, it won't be a problem."*
>
> *"Okay." I slid across the sheet next to him and threw my leg over his hips. We kissed, this time with our lips lightly brushing, tentative and gentle. We did that for quite awhile and I have to admit, it was nice. The next thing I knew, his hard penis was pushing against my leg like a dog fighting a leash. We began to move against each other more vigorously. And somehow I found myself sucking him and he started doing his animal calls.*

Although the sex *talk* here is graphic, we actually don't see much sex. This is more of the implied sex scene with the door closing in the reader's face. Notice that the boldness of the sex talk comes from Blue. She's trying to shock Rush, test him a little. She's just come from a devastating meeting with her parents, free after twenty years in prison, during which they revealed to her that as a little girl, she had unwittingly led the FBI to them and, therefore, was responsible for them being imprisoned. She feels guilty here, unworthy of love, so she tries to push away the one man who's been kindest to her.

For me, the romance of the scene takes place through the dialogue. I find dialogue to be the most attractive (and sexiest) feature in a person because it reveals that person's intelligence and character. As they banter back and forth, snapping at each other but also being open with each other, I'm trying to show that the sparring is bringing them closer and closer. In fact, I deliberately went against convention and gave him a less than erect penis. That was for two reasons: (1) to show he wasn't after her just for sex—that her verbal cruelty was getting to him; and (2) to show he was man enough not to be intimidated by the physical situation—he wasn't embarrassed but remained focused on their relationship. Of course, no romantic scene works without the context of the previous pages, which leads up to this payoff moment. In this case, the previous hundred pages showed them together several times, each time their relationship evolving. When the sex scene occurs, they are bringing in their history together as a third character in the room.

Final Word

Some writers prefer to include more romance, while others prefer more sex. Those on both sides enjoy complaining about the other side. Those who indulge in the more reserved romantic writing generally describe their antagonists as being sex-obsessed perverts pandering to the base tastes of sweaty men. The other side thinks of those who focus on romance as unrealistic prudes pandering to the false and harmful hopes of adolescent girls. Or as D.H. Lawrence said, "And what's romance? Usually, a nice little tale where you have everything As You Like It, where rain never wets your jacket and gnats never bite your nose and it's always daisy time." However, most good contemporary writers dabble in both kinds, choosing whatever is appropriate to that particular scene and those particular characters.

I enjoy writing sex scenes because it's always a challenge.

TIP

Sex Quiz

Here's a paragraph from a student's novel. Pick out the phrase that doesn't fit and why.

Linda stared at *Intrepid's* wake from the after sundeck—still lost in a dark corner of her childhood memory. She stood casually, resting her elbows on the shiny teak rail—ankles crossed. Her curvaceous, athletic figure strained at the seams of her designer jeans. Silk-fine, straight blond hair curled just enough at the end to touch the upturned collar of the matching jacket. Linda's well-proportioned, but perky breasts strained only slightly at her white broadcloth shirt. Ornate blue and gold anchors adorned her left shirt pocket and both button-down collars.

If you selected the phrase, "Linda's well-proportioned, but perky breasts strained...," you are correct. He's already told us she is "curvaceous," so the sudden focus on her "perky breasts" pulls the reader out of the story to the author's own leering. Perky breasts would only fit in if there was some reason to focus on them, such as another character's desire for her or her own satisfaction with her figure.

They are some of the most difficult scenes to write. Each scene contains the same basic actions—there's only so many variations, at least that I'm willing to write about—but each time it has to appear fresh, energetic, compelling and often touching. For me, the power of the sex or romantic scene comes after the sex or embrace. It's what the characters do immediately after they've gotten what they wanted that reveals the content of their character. This is why I rarely write the closed door sex scene. The suspense of such a scene isn't in the sexual act; it's in waiting to see how they will interact afterward. What will they say and do? That is where the real romance is.

Instant Workshop:
How Sexy Should It Be?

Maybe you still aren't sure just how explicit a sex scene should be. To decide, you have to figure out how you want the readers to *feel* (not think) as they're reading the scene. Here's a helpful guide. Which kind of sex scene (implied, modest, explicit) would be appropriate to elicit the desired effect? While reading this scene, readers should feel an immediate desire to:

   a. rush over and kiss their significant other.
   b. have passionate sex as soon as possible or dive into a cold swimming pool.
   c. give their significant other a full-body massage until he or she falls asleep in contentment.
   d. take their significant other to a restaurant and movie.
   e. want to phone that old boyfriend or girlfriend they haven't seen in years.
   f. question whether or not their sexual morality is too conventional.

Answers: implied sex scene (d, e); modest sex scene (a, c); explicit sex scene (b, f).

※ 13 ※
THE LONG GOOD-BYE:
FINAL SCENES

"Ends always give me trouble. Characters run away with you, and so won't fit on to what is coming."

E.M. Forster

*"We are driven
By endings as by hunger. We must know
How it comes out, the shape o' the whole...."*

A.S. Byatt

When the classic film *Chinatown* was released to rave reviews, one of the aspects that everyone praised was the brutal but realistic ending. On the dark streets of Los Angeles's Chinatown, the love interest (Faye Dunaway) is shot dead through the eye while trying to save her daughter from her powerful, incestuous father (John Huston). Dunaway's daughter, the product of Dunaway's father raping his own daughter, witnesses the shooting. While she screams in horror, the evil but politically powerful father comes over to hug and comfort her, and the audience knows that the sexual abuse that happened to the mother/daughter will happen to the daughter/granddaughter. The private detective hero (Jack Nicholson) is outraged and starts after the evil father, but Jack's partner holds him back and says, "Forget it, Jake. It's Chinatown." Meaning, of course, that in the real world, for which Chinatown is a metaphor, there's no way to fight the rich and powerful. Pretty grim ending, especially for Hollywood, where conventional wisdom states that an unhappy ending costs the film anywhere from ten to twenty million dollars at the box office. However, *Chinatown*'s honesty and refusal to pander made it a critical and financial success. (Though, who knows? If Jake had saved Faye Dunaway and killed the evil father, it might have made even more money.)

After the film came out, the screenwriter, Robert Towne, complained about the ending. He had written a happier ending and was angry that director Roman Polanski had changed it. "That's not the ending I wrote," he said to interviewers. Polanski's response was, "No, but this ending is unforgettable." Last year, Towne was asked whether he still thought Polanski's ending was the wrong one. This time he said no, he now saw that it was the better ending.

What have we learned from this? First, an ending should be unforgettable. Second, as a writer, you must be flexible.

Taking the Last Shot

The last scene of a story or novel has a special burden. A great ending can make a mediocre story seem better; a mediocre ending can make an otherwise powerful story seem disappointing. It's like that clichéd scene we see so often in movies: The basketball players are moving down the court in slow motion, three seconds left in the game, one point behind. The ball is passed to our hero, who launches himself up for a half-court jump shot. The ball arcs up, up, up, then drops down, down, down. It rolls around the rim of the basket a few times and...

Whatever.

No matter how great they played throughout the entire game, it all comes down to this last shot. The game is won or lost in that final three-second "scene." This does not mean that a story or novel is ultimately good or bad depending upon the last scene, but it greatly affects how the reader perceives his experience with the work. How many times have you come to the end of a story, novel, play or movie, only to shake your head in frustration and disappointment? You feel let down and a bit foolish for having wasted all that time and money on a story that barely limped across the finish line. It's even worse when the first half of the story was so promising.

Why is the phenomenon of the bad ending so widespread?

A well-known director said that making a movie is like taking a stagecoach ride through the Old West: At first you hope for a pleasant journey filled with wonderful sights and exciting people, but halfway through, you just want to get the hell to where you're going! Writing is like that. Writers often are so excited to finally be nearing the finish that they tend to rush the ending. I made this same mistake many times at the beginning of my career. I would slavishly craft every word for the first 95 percent of the story, then in a white-hot rush of adrenaline, I'd gobble down the last 5 percent. It would take me a year to write two hundred pages of a novel, but I would finish the last fifty in two days of nonstop writing. And it showed.

Beginning writers often think that it's okay to write quickly at the end—to "get it all out on paper"—because they can fix it later. What they mean is that they can fix the style later, polish the prose, add nice metaphors and descriptions, tweak the dialogue. That's sometimes true, but generally that's not what's wrong with the endings. It's like starting with a spoiled piece of beef and saying you can fix the flavor with spices. Indeed you can, but those who eat it will still get sick. The problem often comes because the author has not spent enough time *thinking* about the ending. Forget the writing for a moment; put down the pen and shut off the computer. Spend some time just thinking through the variations of what might happen and what effect each variation will have on the reader.

I get both elated and scared when I come to the end of a novel. Elated because it will soon be over; scared because I'm afraid I'll blow it all. That's why every day, sometimes for a couple of weeks, I think things through, ask myself questions about what the characters should do and would do and sketch out the various scenarios. All in an effort to make the ending seem like the fulfillment of the story.

There's only one definite rule about endings: *An ending must seem inevitable without being predictable.* Read that line again—it's important.

"Inevitable without being predictable" means that when the reader arrives at the end of the story, he must read the last words and feel satisfied that this is the only way the story could have ended. Yet, he shouldn't feel that he knew all along that this would happen. Obviously, some endings are predictable in that the reader knows the girl will get the boy or the bad guys will be defeated. In such cases, the ending isn't about *what* happens, it's about *how* it happens. How does the girl get the boy? How are the bad guys defeated? Especially when the ending is known, the reader is counting on you to make it surprising.

For me, the ending is like arriving at the end of a dimly lit tunnel and flipping a light switch. When you look back, you can see what the tunnel looked like for the first time. So, too, in a story. The ending should cast a light on all of the pages that you've written and illuminate them for the first time.

The Difference Between Endings in Short Stories and Novels

First, we need to make some technical distinctions. The final scene in a story is different than in a novel. In a story, the final scene may be only a few paragraphs, an addendum or continuation of action from the climactic scene. In a novel, the final scene is often a separate chapter after the climax and may include several scenes. In a story, the final scene is generally punchier, insistent, more like the last lines of a poem. You need to end with an emotional and/or intellectual jab. In a novel, the final scene tends to be a wrap-up, bringing the larger scope of events into clearer focus. It's usually less intense (the intensity having come from the climax), but still has a great deal of impact. The ending of a novel tells the reader how to feel and what to think about the events that just happened. It is more like a debriefing: gathering people who've been through an intense emotional experience and talking them through it so they can gain greater perspective on what just happened.

Coming to a Bad End

Whenever I go around the classroom collecting my students' short stories, I already know one thing for sure: 90 percent of the endings will be bad. Very bad. This is not because they are bad writers; in fact, many of the stories are exceptional—until the ending. For the most part, the endings are too predictable. The reader can see where it's going long before he arrives at the ending. It's like hearing a long, involved joke when you already know the punchline. Beginning writers need to take into account that endings are not merely an interchangeable convention, a one-size-fits-all bin where they can slap on anything from the top shelf and it will be fine. The cure for this is twofold: (1) Read, read, read. As with any art form, the more the artist is exposed to what others are doing—whether painting, music or dance—the more the artist is aware of the possibilities and parameters of that art form. Not only will you be exposed to endings that work, but you will be more sensitive to endings that don't work and why. (2) Push, push, push. Push yourself past the tidy, familiar endings, and start creating endings that are customized to your particular story.

There are a few categories of conventional endings that are so common, they have names. They are distinguished by their predictable and disappointing nature. Do not befriend or feed them, or they will hang around and devour your story. Among the breeds to avoid:

No-Ending Ending

This is when the story just abruptly ends and you keep turning the page wondering if there's a page missing from your copy. You suspect that there must be a deeper meaning that you just aren't getting because why else would the person end the story here? Of course, it's possible that there's a deeper meaning, but it's just as possible that the writer couldn't figure out how to resolve the story and just hoped it would be enough.

However, even though an ending may not seem to resolve the conflicts of the story, that doesn't mean it's a no-ending ending. The author may have left the ending hanging to tell the reader that there was no resolution for these characters.

Twilight Zone Ending

As much as I enjoyed the old Rod Serling TV series, as a writer and reader, I sometimes curse its influence on budding writers. Rather than compose an ending that evolves out of the conflicts their characters have faced, they slip in a twist to the ending that they obviously think will give their story some depth or at least entertainment value. Wrong on both counts. The twist ending offers no depth because it is a contrivance that roughly elbows its way into the story. Everything that came before is reduced to mere setup for this "punch line" ending. The characters are no longer important and all of the reader's time spent caring about what happens to them is sacrificed on the altar of "Surprise!" True, there could be some entertainment in terms of the shock value, but that is generally short-lived and once again reduces the rest of the story to an elaborate artifice to support the twist. The main problem with counting on the shock value is that it would have to accomplish two things: (1) truly take the reader by surprise, and (2) not seem too contrived. Considering the number of plots the average reader is exposed to through the various media, it would be an extremely rare twist that actually surprised him. As for contrivances, the twist ending is by nature artificial, pulling the reader out of the story to marvel at the ending as if it were a sideshow freak.

What's especially annoying about this kind of ending is the intrusion of the writer's smug sense of being clever. For example, there are many stories in which someone wishes for something, only to have a demonic presence give that person what they wished for but in some punishingly literal manner that only torments that individual for eternity. In the famous "The Monkey's Paw" story by W.W. Jacobs, a mother wishes for her dead son to come back, only he comes back as a corpse. This has no insight into the nature of our wishes or fantasies; instead, it suggests that satanic demons are basically really strict grammarians, eager to punish a slip of syntax.

THIS-REALLY-HAPPENED ENDING

Sometimes writers present a bland or unbelievable ending, which they justify by saying, "But this really happened to me." Stories aren't about facts; they're about truth. Save the facts for your diary. Rather, ask what truths are revealed by those facts (meaning plot). To examine why certain events took place, ask how the characters got themselves into such a situation, then—before deciding on whether to end with what really happened or to devise an ending of your own—consider what that ending has to say about the characters and the situation.

POETIC JUSTICE ENDING

Let's say a villain decides to kill someone by injecting him with a lethal virus. He sneaks up on the guy, syringe poised, needle only inches from the victim's neck. Suddenly a door opens, bumping the villain's arm and forcing the needle into the villain's own chest. Beginning writers love this kind of ending because it's so tidy. And ironic. "Look, it's ironic," they say. To which one responds, "So?" Irony is one of the lowest levels of payoff. It seems contrived and phony and is disappointing to the reader.

TIGER-OR-THE-LADY ENDING

There's a famous short story by Frank Stockton entitled "The Tiger, or the Lady?" in which the hero is placed in front of two doors. Behind one is a hungry tiger that will devour him; behind the other is a beautiful lady who will become his lover. Only he doesn't get to choose the door—his lover does. This is the punishment for their illicit love. The story ends with the reader not knowing which door his lover chose: Did she choose the lady, knowing her lover would then live with this other woman, or the tiger, deciding to kill him rather than give him to another woman? This is the hanging ending because it leaves the reader wondering what will happen next. This is another favorite of beginning writers because it saves them the agony and hard work of actually coming up with a good ending. The reader does not want to commit himself to caring about characters only to have the writer cheese out by leaving the ending up to the reader. If a reader wanted to choose endings, he'd write his own stories and not read yours.

YOU-FIGURE-IT-OUT ENDING

Also known as the huh ending because you just stare, scratch your head and say, "Huh?" This ending is so obscure and unintelligible that you're tempted to think it must be meaningful, as with the no-ending ending. *The Blair Witch Project* is a spooky little film with a lot of good characterization and suspense, but the ending is so undecipherable that no one knows exactly what happened. The problem with such an ending is that the focus then is on the puzzle aspect of the story, and figuring it out becomes a game. This treats your characters and plot as if they were nothing more than an elaborate crossword puzzle, easily disposable.

Coming to a Good End

Now that you know what kind of endings to avoid, let's look at an ending that works and why. John Updike's story, "A&P," is about a nineteen-year-old boy dissatisfied with his life, which consists of working as a cashier in the A&P grocery store of a small beach town. Sammy is not an overly thoughtful boy, not really aware of the cause of his dissatisfaction, though the reader quickly realizes he's afraid that this job and this store are basically the rest of his life, as it is for his co-workers. To him, the A&P represents an overly structured society in which most people are merely robotically fulfilling the expectations of others, never really knowing who they are or what they're capable of becoming (like the people living in pods in the movie *The Matrix*). When the story starts, Sammy is a card-carrying member of the A&P, upholder of their values. Then three pretty girls walk in wearing only bathing suits and Sammy starts to see things differently. He sees how everyone reacts to them, from the "houseslaves in pin curlers" to the employees, with disapproval. When the store manager, Lengel, comes over and tells the girls that they have to come in decently dressed, Sammy intuitively realizes that he's not part of the A&P crowd. Sammy reacts, which sets up the story's ending.

> *The girls, and who'd blame them, are in a hurry to get out, so I say "I quit" to Lengel quick enough for them to hear, hoping they'll stop and watch me, their unsuspected hero. They keep right on going, into the electric eye; the door flies open and they flicker across the lot to their car, Queenie and Plaid and Big Tall Goony-Gooney (not that as raw material she was so bad), leaving me with Lengel and a kink in his eyebrow.*
>
> *"Did you say something, Sammy?"*
>
> *"I said I quit."*
>
> *"I thought you did."*
>
> *"You didn't have to embarrass them."*
>
> *"It was they who were embarrassing us."*
>
> *I started to say something that came out "Fiddle-de-doo." It's a saying of my grandmother's, and I know she would have been pleased.*
>
> *"I don't think you know what you're saying," Lengel said.*
>
> *"I know you don't," I said. "But I do." I pull the bow at the back of my apron and start shrugging it off my shoulders. A*

couple customers that had been heading for my slot begin to knock against each other, like scared pigs in a chute.

Lengel sighs and begins to look very patient and old and gray. He's been a friend of my parents for years. "Sammy, you don't want to do this to your Mom and Dad," he tells me. It's true, I don't. But it seems to me that once you begin a gesture it's fatal not to go through with it. I fold the apron, "Sammy" stitched in red on the pocket, and put it on the counter, and drop the bow tie on top of it. The bow tie is theirs, if you've ever wondered. "You'll feel this for the rest of your life," Lengel says, and I know that's true, too, but remembering how he made that pretty girl blush makes me so scrunchy inside I punch the No Sale tab and the machine whirs "pee-pul" and the drawer splats out. One advantage to this scene taking place in summer, I can follow this up with a clean exit, there's no fumbling around getting your coat and galoshes, I just saunter into the electric eye in my white shirt my mother ironed the night before, and the door heaves itself open, and outside the sunshine is skating around on the asphalt.

I look around for my girls, but they're gone, of course. There wasn't anybody but some young married screaming with her children about some candy they didn't get by the door of a powder-blue Falcon station wagon. Looking back in the big windows, over the bags of peat moss and aluminum lawn furniture stacked on the pavement, I could see Lengel in my place in the slot, checking the sheep through. His face was dark gray and his back stiff, as if he'd just had an injection of iron, and my stomach kind of fell as I felt how hard the world was going to be to me hereafter.

The ending scene is divided into three distinct sections: (1) The Act, which is Sammy quitting; (2) The Fallout, which are the immediate results of The Act; and (3) The Reconciliation, in which Sammy comes to reconcile his act with the larger picture. Here's how it all works together:

The Act. The first paragraph has Sammy quitting while the girls are still standing there. This plot development takes the reader by surprise because Sammy has given no indication that he is the kind of kid who would do something so drastic on principle. Yet, looking back over the story, the reader can see a progression within him that evolves from vague dissatisfaction to an awareness that the people in the A&P have accepted their roles in society without questioning them. This is what existentialists call "the herd instinct," the desire to adopt rules of behavior rather than take responsibility for choosing paths of right and wrong. (That existential concept is the theme of the story, with the A&P representing a type of Eden from which Sammy is self-expelled.) When the reader looks back on those moments that show Sammy's progression, he can see that quitting, though unpredictable, was inevitable.

Notice that the girls leave. This is important because now Sammy has to make his decision *again*—this time without any hope of the material reward of having the girls appreciate his gesture. The girls may have inspired his spontaneous gesture, but now he has to decide based on the merits of the gesture itself.

Updike undercuts the seriousness of the situation by having Sammy still judging them physically. He's progressed from the sexist adolescent in the beginning of the story, who wonders if girls really have minds or just a jar in their heads that contains a buzzing bee. This is more realistic: Personal enlightenment is a long road, each step made through the choices we make. Sammy's still a kid, but one for whom the reader has hope.

Updike also uses a good descriptive line: "...leaving me with Lengel and a kink in his eyebrow." Rather than use an obvious description such as, "Lengel fumed" or "Lengel glared angrily," Updike uses an image, which makes the moment more visual and, therefore, has more impact.

The Fallout. The conversation between Lengel and Sammy is stark, with Lengel's responses presented in the monotone of the self-anointed. Sammy doesn't cave in to Lengel's moral pressure and takes his apron off. Removing the apron is the shrugging off of the social uniform of conformity he's had to wear. Naturally, when he does this, the other customers react like "scared pigs in a chute" or the herd of conformers that they are. (This is not a story saying that social conventions are wrong and anarchy rules. Rather, it's saying that accepting convention without question is wrong because it limits your options of who you might become.)

Once Sammy makes his decision—without any hope of reward from the girls—Lengel "begins to look very patient and old and gray." This isn't saying that Lengel necessarily changes, but that Sammy begins to see Lengel this way. Sammy's perception of the world has already started to change as a result of his action. The description of Lengel is also meant to echo that of a traditional image of God, perhaps the one in the Sistine Chapel. Sammy's rejection of Lengel is a rejection of the conventional perception of God, who demands that humans follow certain rules, and an embracing of self-reliance in deciding moral right and wrong.

Lengel pulls out two more cards to play: "Sammy, you don't want to do this to your Mom and Dad," and "You'll feel this for the rest of your life." Sammy agrees but is willing to take the risk that comes with independent thought. His response is: "But it seems to me that once you begin a gesture it's fatal not to go through with it." The key word choice here is "fatal," meaning death. Once you determine what the right path is and you back down from taking it, you're killing a small part of yourself. And then it becomes easier to back down each time until you've murdered the person you might have become and are ready for your place among the pigs in a chute.

Updike deliberately wants Sammy not to be too educated or articulate (hence, the many grammatical errors in Sammy's point of view) because making the right choice isn't a matter of external learning. It's a matter of listening to the intuitive part of yourself that wants to survive, not be killed off one piece at a time. That's why Sammy doesn't explain why he quit in intellectual terms, but merely says, "but remembering how he made that pretty girl blush makes me so scrunchy inside...." "Scrunchy" is his intuitive self speaking.

This section ends with another strong visual image: "in my white shirt that my mother ironed the night before...." The shirt is white not just because that's what the employees of the A&P wear (if it were the only reason, there'd be no need to mention it, especially here); it's white because it symbolizes Sammy's innocence, which is coming to an end. Also, the added detail that his mother ironed it for him reminds us that what he's leaving isn't just the job, but the state of dependence in which a nineteen-year-old still has his mother ironing his shirts.

The Reconciliation. The final paragraph is where Sammy has to reconcile his actions with what they mean to his life. When he steps out of the A&P, he sees that the girls are gone, "of course." The "of course" tells us that he wasn't really expecting to see them, that his decision had nothing to do with them. He sees "some young married screaming with her children about some candy they didn't get by the door of a powder-blue Falcon station wagon." Again, he uses a visual image to tell us something: This woman and her child screaming for candy represents what he's leaving behind—the preprogrammed, materialistic world of the A&P.

But the story doesn't end there. Sammy looks back into the window and sees Lengel in Sammy's old cashier slot, "checking the sheep through." The story then does an unexpected twist—not the contrived twist of the Twilight Zone ending—but a twist that is realistic and, therefore, more powerful: "and my stomach kind of fell as I felt how hard the world was going to be to me hereafter." Instead of ending with Sammy's triumphant exit, the story lingers, has him look back and see Lengel. His stomach falls because he realizes how easily replaced he was. The world of the A&P doesn't care about his gestures; it goes on as it always has. The reward isn't in getting the girls or even in having that great I-beat-the-system feeling. Rather, Sammy realizes that the world is indifferent to his moral triumph and the reward is the act itself. The last word, "hereafter," picks up on that kicked-out-of-Eden theme discussed earlier, but Sammy accepts that life is harder if you choose to eat from the tree of the knowledge of good and evil and decide these things for yourself.

As you can see, a lot is going on in what seems like a straightforward ending. The skilled writer tries to utilize every line of dialogue, description and interior monologue to elicit as much emotion and meaning as possible. This is accomplished by focusing on who the characters are and what they want, and how that relates to what they finally get. If we could ask the Sammy at the beginning of the story what he wanted out of life, we'd get a different answer than we would from the Sammy at the end of the story. Yet, the Sammy at the end of the story is happier, more mature and more confident because he got something unexpected.

Now let's look at some sections of the final chapter in *Lessons in Survival*. This ending is a little different for me because I jump ahead two years after the previous scene—a comical bank robbery—which is the plot climax scene. The function of this last scene is to show the effect of all the plot events on the protagonist, Blue Erhardt. Each of the sections of the novel has a title that is taken from some common direction we might see during the day, for example, "Do Not Shake. Contents Under Pressure." These titles serve as "lessons" because each of these mundane phrases takes on a double meaning when applied to the characters. The final chapter has its own title, "Exact Change Required," which tells the reader that this scene is about those changes. Also, though the rest of the book is written in past tense, the last chapter is written in present tense in order to emphasize that her past is a thing of the past. She's a different woman in the present.

> *The universe is in a constant state of flux. Yet nothing changes.*
>
> *Two years ago I robbed a Los Angeles bank dressed as my mother and then anointed Manhattan Beach with a trail of my urine. Today I am driving home from school next to a stack of eleventh grade essays on "Those Remarkable Intestines." I pop the glove compartment and dig out a Baby Ruth, tearing it open with my teeth and chomping into it with great anticipation of that exquisite first tang of chocolate on my tongue.*
>
> *I am no longer a celebrity. My fifteen minutes ended when the movie came out. Nothing happened as we'd expected.*
>
> *I turn the corner onto my street, a pleasant cul-de-sac of detached homes in the moderate price range. Realtors call them "starter homes," because they're the only thing a lot of young couples starting out can afford. Most of the couples who live in this neighborhood are younger than I. Their yards are weighted down with tricycles and dog shit. In the summer Peter from next door and Justin from down the street, both ten this*

year, set up a lemonade stand and charge $1 a glass. They sell very few glasses. Justin wants to lower the price and do more volume. But Peter always convinces him that it is classier to sell fewer glasses for more money. It makes me happy to know that this debate of economic philosophy will probably continue for at least another two summers. And each summer I will buy my usual glass once a week on my Sunday jog.

I park at the curb because there's not enough room in the garage, but I'll get to the reason why in a minute. First, I check the mail. The mail box is a custom job, looks like a lizard with his mouth open. A gift from Rush. He painted the eyes blood-shot.

Bills. Ads. Magazines. Nothing from my parents. I haven't seen them since our clandestine rendezvous three months ago in Montana. They were working at a dude ranch there, calling themselves Nadine and Dwayne. Mom had black hair and looked like Joan Jett. She barbecued for the guests. Dad had lost some weight and stopped smoking. He still knew how to handle a horse, though, and he did some showing off for us that I knew would cost him a long night with a heating pad. Still, we applauded from atop the corral and he waved his cowboy hat at us as he rode another lap.

Mom and I went for a walk along the creek and argued about the upcoming presidential elections. I had never heard of the candidate she was supporting.

"How do you like my hair, Mom?" I asked.

"What? It's nice."

"Not too long?"

She shook her head. "It's fine."

I laughed. Some of my friends complained that their mothers constantly picked on them for being too fat or thin or dowdy or showy. Hairstyle seemed the favorite battleground. Mom had never been like that. She worried over my mind, but she never had a need to criticize me. I only recently realized the difference.

She stooped by the river and plucked a flower.

I laughed. "You're picking flowers, Mom. This is starting to look like a douche commercial. For those days when you don't feel...fresh."

"TV commercials destroy any confidence a woman has in herself. They convince her that without exterior products she is incapable of being attractive or sustaining a relationship." She waved a disgusted hand. "Don't get me started."

I plucked a flower just like Mom's.

"You know what this is?" she asked. "What kind?"

"No," I said.

"Me neither." She laughed and stuck it in her hair. She took mine and stuck it in my hair. "The douche twins," she said and laughed so hard her flower fell out of her hair. At that moment she was the most perfect mom in the world and I wished we'd never stop walking along this river.

Mom and Dad left Montana six weeks ago and I have no idea where they are. They haven't written or called, they can't. The FBI is still after them. But they manage to get messages to me on occasion through friends. Plus I get to read their words every couple months in Rolling Stone. My parents are writers now, penning articles about "Underground America." A counterculture travelogue describing places they've been, their observations about the people in those places. At the beginning of each article is a boxed disclaimer from Rolling Stone management informing the reader that Harold and Naomi Henderson are fugitives and that the magazine does not pay them for these articles, printing them only as a matter of public record and information. However, Dad told me once that someone at the magazine managed to get a few bucks to them now and then through third parties.

I take my key out and unlock the front door. I have to jiggle the key a bit to get it out of the lock again. Another thing to add to the list of what needs fixed around here. It would have to wait until next month's paycheck. Things are a little tight now. That's not the way it was supposed to be, I know, what with the movie deal and all.

She then goes on to describe all the crazy things that happened with the movie deal, which we'll skip. What the reader has so far, though, is Blue cataloguing the changes in her life from the last time he saw her. The reader discovers she's back teaching high school biology, which is what she was doing when the novel began. And she's living in the same kind of community she was when the novel opened. The difference here is tone—she likes what she does and where she lives, she feels comfortable now where before she felt as if she were hiding from life. The flower-picking scene with her mother is included because it echoes an earlier scene, a childhood flashback in which her mother teaches her the names of flowers as they take walks. The "douche twins" joke may seem vulgar, but it's here to show that Blue is no longer in awe of her mother or feels overshadowed by her. They laugh together at a stupid joke. For me, a touching moment is when the father continues to show off his horse riding even though he knows he'll pay for it the next day. I included this because Blue needed to see her father sacrificing himself for her, just as he used to for Big Causes. That, too, is reconciliation. And there's a little suspense hook about her "telling" us later.

We'll skip ahead to the last few pages of the chapter. In the section not included here, Blue reveals she's married to Rush, the independent producer wannabe with whom she's been having an on-again/off-again relationship throughout the book. When we enter the chapter again, Rush is videotaping Blue as she enters their—surprise!—baby daughter's room.

"Here she is," Rush says, pointing his camera down at the crib and circling slowly. "Here's Mommy."

I picked up my daughter and kissed her cheeks and forehead. "Hello, Amelia. Is Amelia getting as tired of Daddy's Alfred Hitchcock impression as Mommy? Hmmm?"

"Hold that look!" Rush says zooming in on my face. He lowers the camera, kisses Amelia, then kisses me, then brings the camera back up.

People think of happiness, I think, as a place you visit. Like a vacation in Hawaii or Disney World. Two weeks in Happiness, then back to real life. That's wrong.

I'm guessing now, because I'm a little short on scientific evidence. But I say happiness is the state of not expecting, not anticipating, not waiting for things to happen. Not waiting for your life to start.

Thomas Q was right. It's all been said before. We are des-

tined to be born just as ignorant of ourselves as the cave people were of themselves. And every word we utter, every thought we have, every feeling we experience, every insight we relish from birth to death will have been thought, felt, experienced, and relished before us. And none of it will make any difference. Is anything lonelier than knowing that?

The thing is, so what? People spend a lot of time worrying about their flaws. They diet, exercise, dress up, pray. We're afraid of the imperfections in each other, they threaten us. They could be contagious. People want to be perfect. I don't think people are flawed. Calling them flaws is a moralist's language, not a biologist's. Biology sees no flaws—every living organism is perfect, flawless. Existence is the proof of perfection. Because once a species becomes anything less than perfect, it fails to survive. Love is part of our survival technique. We need it to survive. If we don't accept that, we become extinct.

I never finished my thesis on Thomas Q. I never finished my religion degree. Three weeks after the robbery, when The Bend had been evacuated of all guests and staff, the whole place burned to the ground. Thomas Q was never found, though his personal effects—watch, wallet, keys—were found in the rubble. Since there was no one to claim the insurance money, it went to a secondary beneficiary, a small Methodist college in Pennsylvania. They built a football stadium with it, which made me laugh for a few days.

Once Rush got mad thinking about Thomas Q. Rush has this thing about free will. "The bastard manipulated all of us like puppets. I'm not complaining about the results, I'm satisfied about that. But I just hate the idea of how he did it. We all ended up doing exactly what he wanted us to do. What right did he have to play God?"

"Because we let him," I said.

A month after Amelia was born, a package arrived from Singapore. It was a wooden paddle with a rubber ball attached by an elastic string. No note.

"Who do you love more, Amelia, Mommy or Daddy?" Rush says, filming.

"Rush, don't ask her that. She's barely six months old. You'll traumatize her."

"*Afraid of the answer, huh?*"

"*I smell a bet.*"

"*Three changes,*" *he suggests.*

"*Deal.*"

We shake hands. This is an old game with us. We each say our name (to Amelia, Daddy and Mommy are our names), and whichever one she makes a significant noise after is the winner. All our bets consist of the same thing, the number of diaper changes the other has to do solo. Rush owes six changes already which is why he's so anxious to bet.

We lean over the crib.

"*Mommy,*" *I sing.*

Amelia looks over at the window.

"*Daddy,*" *Rush says, making a goofy face.*

Amelia pulls my hair.

Back and forth we go, getting no reaction.

Mitzi is still acting. After a two-month campaign for the role of Dulcinea, she's playing Don Quixote's sister in Man of La Mancha. *Rush showed her how to let the air out of the theater director's car tires, which she did twice already. Apparently her terrorist attacks are working because the director promised her the role of Maria in* The Sound of Music.

Kyra is attending the local university and babysitting for us on occasion. She still dresses in bib overalls and Keds. She's had an offer from a publisher for her Terms of Endearment *collection, which has doubled in size. Also, she has a boyfriend who Mitzi and I are convinced will break her heart.*

"*There,*" *Rush says.* "*I win.*"

"*That's drooling, which doesn't count as an affirmative sound. Mommmyyyy.*"

Amelia's eyes droop, open wide, then close. She is asleep. I kiss her on the forehead and smell her skin. I can never get too much of her smell.

Rush lifts his camera again and starts filming.

"*You forfeit,*" *I say.*

"*She's asleep, for God's sake.*"

"*She fell asleep after hearing my name and before hearing yours. In anticipation of hearing yours she nodded off. I rest my case.*"

"You're a worse lawyer than I was."

"Okay, it's a tie." I press my cheek against Amelia and close my eyes. Having a baby did not make me happy. Nor did marrying Rush. Not being afraid to do either made me happy.

When I open my eyes Rush is circling Amelia and me, filming again. He gets in these filming moods every so often. I suppose I should be annoyed, but he is such an enthusiastic father that I don't mind.

"I'm going for that mother-daughter bonding thing here, Blue," he says. "Act happy."

"What?" Act happy? The words strike me as funny.

"Act happy," he repeats.

I start to laugh. I can't stop, I don't want to stop.

"I said act happy, not insane," Rush says. But he is laughing too.

Amelia wakes up and starts crying. I bounce her in my arms, but I am still laughing. Amelia stops crying and stares at me blankly. "Mommy," I say to her and she giggles and waves her arms and legs. "Mommy," I say again and she rocks her head side to side, squealing and giggling and drooling onto my sweater. "I win," I tell Rush.

Rush lays the camera on the changing table. He comes over and wraps his arms around Amelia and me. We kind of sway there. He looks at Amelia and says, "Mommy's a cheater. Did you know that about her?"

"So what?" I say.

And we sway in a cradle of arms and dropped food for the dust mites who celebrate below.

Some of the above section tells what happened to other characters whom the reader came to know. The most important character, Thomas Q, is a likable spiritual leader who did indeed manipulate things so that Rush and Blue ended up together, though only Blue realizes that part. In fact, I intended for him to be a godlike character who creates a *deus ex machina* to bring the lovers together (see "Romantic Comedy" in chapter eleven). By the way, the package she gets from Singapore tells Blue that Thomas Q is still alive.

The last few paragraphs focus on Rush, Blue and their

daughter. The wagering of diaper changes between the parents is meant to illustrate Blue's relaxed nature, very different from the Blue at the beginning of the novel. It also shows the closeness between her and Rush. The laughter that erupts from Blue over the concept of "act happy" is there for the reader to slow down and remember that acting happy is how Blue had spent her life—acting for everyone. Now she's no longer acting, which is why she's laughing.

The final sentence, separated into its own paragraph for emphasis, is meant to provide a strong visual image that ties together the themes. The reference to dust mites recalls the old Blue, who in an earlier chapter was unable to relax during sex because she couldn't stop thinking of the dust mites all around her (see chapter twelve). The reason I made her a biology teacher was to have her obsessed with the endless activity of life around her, making her feel insignificant. This last sentence tells the reader that she no longer cares about the big picture of the endless swirl of life-forms. She's content with what she has: chaotic, messy and fulfilling.

Final Word

Maybe defining a good ending is like the famous definition of pornography: "I know it when I see it." For me, a good ending affects both the emotions and the intellect. I feel, and I think about why I feel. Two movies with great endings immediately come to mind: *Raising Arizona* and *The Third Man*. In *Raising Ari-*

TIP

How to Avoid Rushing Your Ending

Most writers need to maintain a pretty strict writing schedule in order to produce quality pages. That means writing a certain number of hours every day, including revising for a specified number of hours. Try to stick to this same schedule at the end of a story or novel. If you write three hours a day, keep writing that same amount of time, maybe a little more. But then stop! Don't keep going just because you have the energy or time. Instead, make some notes about what you will write tomorrow. It's much better to come back already knowing what you want to write. Plus, the extra time gives you a chance to think about what you intend to write. Sometimes that extra thinking time will allow you to reconsider and maybe come up with a better way to write the ending. Or it will provide you with time to enhance the original idea. Either way, the story is better off.

zona, there's a flash-forward in which Nicolas Cage's character dreams about what the future will be like. It's both touching and funny. In *The Third Man*, the character played by Joseph Cotton stands by the side of the road waiting for a woman he loves (but who loathes him for betraying his friend—Orson Welles—even though the friend was pure evil and betrayed her) as she walks toward him. This last scene echoes one of the opening scenes. Ironically, both are funerals for the same man. Cotton waits...and waits...and waits as she walks down that long road. The audience grows impatient, wondering if she'll stop and reconcile with him. Rent the movie and find out for yourself.

✠ 14 ✠
FROM MESS TO
MASTERPIECE:
STRUCTURING

> *"Style and structure are the essence of a book;*
> *great ideas are hogwash."*
>
> Vladimir Nabokov

> *"The structure of a play is always the story of how*
> *the birds come home to roost."*
>
> Arthur Miller

As with most things in life, being too close to something can distort your perception of it. When you're too close to a person, you may not see that the relationship is destructive. Or that a diet is harmful. Or that a hairstyle is unflattering. Or that your child is a bully. The same thing happens with writing, maybe especially with writing. You work so hard on the minutiae, on choosing every word, every gesture of every character, what they wear, what they say, what they eat and drive and think, that you can't get enough distance to see whether it all goes together as you imagined it would when you first set it on paper. Fortunately, there are a few techniques to help you develop a more realistic perspective.

Visualizing Through Note Cards
One such technique is aerial mapping. Aerial maps are those photographs of cities and other locations taken from up in the air. If you're standing on the streets of New York City with everything rushing around you from all sides, it seems like a

chaotic jumble. But from a mile up, a serene pattern emerges and it all seems to make sense.

CHAPTER: 12

POINT OF VIEW: Karen

CHACTR.: Tommy, security guard (Jim Mahoney), saleswoman (Tina Jaspers)

SETTING: Shopping mall (111): Toys "R" Us (113), Dairy Queen (118)

PLOT:

    1. Karen takes Tommy into Toys "R" Us to buy a b'day present.

    2. Tommy shoplifts a Batman action figure.

    3. Security guard stops K and T as they leave store.

KEY INFO: description of Karen's VW Jetta, how she got the dent in the bumper

PAGES: 110-118 (9 pgs.)

In order to better position your scenes, it's a good idea to use a similar visual method of "seeing" your scenes. I've been using note cards on a bulletin board for years and have found it efficient and effective in helping me better structure a story. It's this simple. Place the following information on a note card: When you see them all lined up on your bulletin board, you have a better idea of the rhythm of the story. Each piece of information on the card is crucial to proper positioning.

- **Point of View:** If the story has multiple points of view, you can look and see that this chapter is from Karen's point of view. When was the last time you used her point of view? Perhaps you should make this chapter thirteen and bring in someone else's point of view first to balance the story.
- **Characters:** This tells you who the major characters are. A hundred pages later when you need to remember the

name of the security guard, you just glance up instead of leafing through the manuscript.

⚜ **Setting:** This is helpful for two reasons. If you write another scene that takes place at Toys "R" Us, you can find the exact page where you first described it (113). This maintains descriptive continuity. Also, it allows you to have an overview of where you are setting scenes to see if you are overusing any one setting. For example, maybe there are too many scenes while a character is driving.

⚜ **Plot:** Seeing the main points of the plot helps you determine which scenes are active and passive. Having three or four scenes in a row of "talking heads" (characters sitting and chatting) can slow the story. You may decide to either change the setting so that instead of sitting at Wendy's discussing their relationship, the characters are grocery shopping for an exotic recipe. This active setting changes the pace but not the purpose of the scene. Or you may decide to add a more active scene between the passive ones. Or you may just move an active scene from somewhere else in the story to this location.

⚜ **Key Information:** This is information you know you'll need to use again later. It could be descriptive or it could be some bit of character information. Being able to locate it at a glance will save you a lot of time.

⚜ **Pages:** You have two pieces of information here, both of which are necessary. The first is the page numbers for the scene. This lets you know where the events are taking place in the grand scheme of the story. You may look up and see that you've waited until halfway through the story to reveal something that should have been revealed earlier. The second number is how many pages the scene takes. When comparing the length of the scenes, you may discover that you have a lot of short or long scenes together and may want to alternate length. Of course, there's nothing wrong with all of the scenes being a similar length, but if you want to expand a particular scene and see that the scenes on either side are short, you may realize that lengthening this one wouldn't hurt the pace.

An additional tip: Use pushpins, not thumbtacks, to hold the note cards in place, and stick them in the bottom of the card, not the top. Then when you get an idea about something you want to add to a previous chapter or scene but you can't work on it for a while, you can jot the idea down and hang it from the pushpin with a binder clip. Sometimes I'll have binder clips full of notes—lines of dialogue, a metaphor, descriptions, maps—hanging from almost every note card.

Using the above note card and bulletin board method of visualizing your story helps you rearrange scenes, find the story's rhythm, heighten suspense and cut the fat. It also helps you (1) keep the whole story in your head as you're writing, and (2) discover any nasty writing habits you may unconsciously be falling prey to. As to the first point, you can glance up at any time as you're writing along and have an instant impression of where the story is and what has happened so far. Don't dismiss that advantage too quickly. It's easy to forget entire scenes when you're busy working on what happens next. And who has time to reread every page every time you sit down to write? The second point may become clear when you look up at that unforgiving board full of note cards. You may see that you seem to like characters talking during car trips because you have three of them in the first thirty pages. Or that you don't like to do your research homework because every scene that requires some, such as a crime scene, is short, cut off by an urgent phone call that allows you to quickly exit the scene.

Rethinking Toward Revising

During my novel and script workshops, I often assign the entire class a novel to read or film to see, after which we outline the story to find its strengths and weaknesses. Once the major scenes are outlined on the dry-erase board, it's easier to see the function of each scene in relation to other scenes and the whole story. Suggestions are then made about how specific scenes might be improved. In a moment, we'll look at a breakdown that a script workshop did of *Entrapment*, the heist thriller starring Sean Connery and Catherine Zeta-Jones. The reason I used this particular film was that it has a combination of good, bland and bad scenes. Plus, it suffers from the same problem that many beginning writers' works suffer from: excellent ideas with lazy execution. Instead of thinking up fresh, vital choices for setting, characterization, plot and dialogue, they often gravitate to the familiar. They think their work is done just by coming up with a catchy premise for the story, but that's when the *real* work begins.

First, we divided the story into its natural three acts. This three-act structure is basic to all storytelling, and you'll find most plots follow this general form.

Act One: Introduces the main characters and core conflict, including plot conflict and character conflict. The plot conflict can be a manifestation of the character conflict. For example, an external plot conflict might be a woman's estranged mother coming back to the small town where she raised her daughter and later abandoned both her husband and daughter. She returns for her husband's funeral. The core conflict is that the daughter is engaged to a terrific local man, but she refuses to set a date for the marriage, claiming she doesn't trust love—look what it did to her family.

Act Two: Complicates the plot by introducing an unexpected plot twist. Just as the estranged mother and daughter are about to reconcile, the mother discovers she has an incurable disease and decides to leave so she's not a burden.

Act Three: Resolves the conflicts, both internal and external. This does not mean that the problems are solved and there is a happy ending; it means that questions raised by the conflicts are answered, even if the characters don't like it. In the example, the daughter discovers that her own inability to marry the local beau isn't because her mother's abandonment makes her believe that love is an illusion and those you love abandon you. Rather, she discovers that her mother did the only thing she could under those circumstances and the daughter subconsciously realizes that if she marries this man, she'll end up doing the same thing.

Okay, that's how it works in general. Here's how it works in specific in *Entrapment*, including an analysis of the main payoff scenes. Before proceeding, I advise you to rent the movie first and see what strengths and weaknesses you discover in each of the three acts. Then match them with the analysis below.

ACT ONE: PAYOFF SCENES
Scene: "Theft of painting"

Purpose: To introduce the brilliance of the thief and misdirect the audience as to the identity of the thief in order to set up later twists.

Analysis: Strong. The theft is exciting because of the dangerous setting (it takes place outside of a high-rise building). The theft is compelling to watch because of the high-tech gadgets and cleverness of the thief in using them to overcome the traps. There is strong suspense, not because the audience fears the thief will be caught (that's never an issue in this scene), but because they see someone watching the thief's every move through a telescope—and don't know who this person is or what he or she will do. Bonus: A humorous "capper" (final line of dialogue or image that is the audience's last impression of the scene) is the replacement of the priceless artwork with a painting of Elvis on velvet.

Grade: A-. The minus is because the theft went too smoothly; even a minor threat that required the thief to cleverly improvise would have raised the adrenaline level a little.

Scene: "The Insurance Investigators"

Purpose: To introduce the antagonists, insurance investigators Catherine Zeta-Jones and her boss, ex-FBI agent Will Patton. To add additional conflict and character motivation by revealing WP has romantic interest in CZJ.

Analysis: Weak. Although CZJ comes across as clever in using computer graphics to show how the thief broke into the "impregnable" room, the scene is flat for a couple of reasons. First, the setting is a busy office filled with people and computers to give the impression of how large the insurance company is and how many resources they have at their disposal. This establishes a Goliath-vs.-David feel: Giant Corporation after little ole Sean Connery (introduced later). However, the setting forces a talking-heads situation with the two characters yammering, giving a huge information dump about SC, the insurance company, their relationship and so on. There's little movement during this scene, so it becomes static and seems to drag. They tried to misdirect the audience from that fact by showing a computer graphic reenactment of how the thief broke in, but the audience has already seen how it was done, so that ploy doesn't work. Instead, they should have introduced these two characters at the scene of the robbery and shown CZJ investigating the room and figuring it out. She could even use the same computer graphics, only now it would be more interesting because it seems as if she's just put it together. The scene appears more active, even though it is only slightly so. Many of my students complained about the introduction of WP's romantic interest in CZJ in this scene. They argued that this subplot should be eliminated. I disagreed. WP's interest in her is important for two reasons: It provides motivation for his dogged pursuit of SC (and CZJ) later, and it demonstrates how she manipulates men to get what she wants. This is a key element to the suspense of whether or not she can manipulate SC, as well as an explanation of how she could work undercover at the insurance agency for five years while being a thief herself. So, yes, keep the element of the romance, but do something with it. The audience never really believes it because the scene only spends a few lines of dialogue to sell it.

Grade: D. It's mostly an information dump in a static setting.

Scene: "CZJ Follows SC"

Purpose: She photographs SC while he uses his cover as a tourist to walk into a high-security lab and steal millions of dollars worth of microchips. This establishes her credentials as the hunter and shows SC in action as a thief.

Analysis: Weak. A general rule of thumb is that any scene in which the audience observes most of the action through a telescopic lens is passive and therefore boring. CZJ watches SC go into the building, time passes, an alarm sounds and the building is cleared. Suddenly, there's SC looking like the confused tourist. A lesson in how to order scenes: This passive sitting-in-the-car scene follows an equally passive sitting-in-the-office scene, making it even more boring, which is a huge blunder in the first third of an action story.

Grade: D+. The passive sit-and-watch scene following a sit-and-talk scene kills the story's momentum, forcing too much pressure on the next scene to jump-start the pace.

Scene: "Naked in Hotel Room"

Purpose: This is a crucial first meeting scene in which the protagonist and antagonist come face to face. She wakes up when she hears a noise, reaches for her gun (only to find it is gone) and sits up, allowing the sheet to slide from her body to reveal her breasts. She sees SC seated across the room with the gun; she makes no effort to cover her exposed breasts. The purpose is to show both characters' strengths: He sneaks into her room without her noticing; she tries to use her charms to manipulate him. He recognizes this about her and asks her if there's ever been a man she hasn't been able to seduce; she says no.

Analysis: Fair. First meetings in which one of the characters is naked is not unusual. In this case, there is the added element that SC set it up so she would have to be naked since he'd broken into her room earlier and stolen all of her clothing. That gives him the advantage in interrogating her. More to the point, she uses her nakedness in trying to persuade him that she's also a thief and she wants him to help her steal a valuable Chinese mask. There are two weaknesses: (1) The dialogue should have been sharper for a first meeting. Both need to be witty and intelligent here, a verbal cat-and-mouse exchange like we've seen in similar stories such as *Charade, To Catch a Thief* and *The Thomas Crown Affair*. Instead, they use the rather clichéd technique of SC saying things like, "Rule number one: Never use a gun. Rule number two...." Why would he be giving her rules? They aren't yet partners, so he's not yet her teacher. (2) His exit from the scene is poorly done. She's talking to him as he steps back into a shadow, then suddenly he's gone. The silliness of that additional cliché undercuts the effect that they just spent a whole scene to achieve.

Grade: B-. A note on the use of nudity in a scene: The audience never sees her breasts, which, in movie terms, are defined as nipples. Despite the disappointment expressed by some students, this was actually a wise storytelling choice. The audience knows that SC can see them and appears to be immune to their allure. If the audience could see them, too, they would distract the audience from the dialogue, which is the crucial element in the scene since it reveals their characters and furthers the plot. Remember the student I mentioned at the end of chapter twelve? In the middle of a serious scene, the author describes the female character physically, ending with "her perky breasts." That phrase completely destroyed the tone of the scene because it was information not coming from the point of view of any of the characters, nor was it information related to the conversation. The perky breasts seemed intrusive, as if the author just wanted to spice the scene up.

Scene: "The Test"

Purpose: SC must test CZJ to make sure she has the skills she claims to have, so he sends her into a seedy store to buy a vase. No matter what happens, she must return with the vase. This will establish the nature of their adversarial relationship: He's the older, wiser guru; she's the brash young, seat-of-her-pants hotshot.

Analysis: An excellent idea, yet weakly executed. Structurally, an action scene is desperately needed here. Notice that the three preceding scenes are all talking-heads scenes (despite the fact that she's naked in one of them). There's still been no real action, even though this film is in the action-thriller genre. There are two parts to this scene: CZJ in the shop getting the vase and the ensuing car chase. The problem with the first part is that when she goes into the shop and tries to buy the vase, the salesman gets aggressive with her for reasons my class had trouble figuring out. I'm sure the reason is there, but not clearly enough. In other words, the conflict between them seems contrived. Of course, the audience knows that something will go wrong because SC gave her explicit directions of what to do. What makes such a scene so delicious is the anticipation of what will go wrong and how it will be resolved (promise and payoff). She resolves the situation by smashing the vase over the salesman's head, thereby discovering the hidden microfilm. When she returns to the car without the vase and SC begins to rant, she grins and shows him the microfilm. The problem is that she accidentally found the microfilm, revealing no cleverness or intelligence on her part (or the part of the writers). The second part of the payoff—the car chase—is adequate. It's the familiar reckless driving down narrow streets while bystanders scatter. Nothing unexpected.

Grade: C+. A terrific idea that spirals into coincidence and clichés.

ACT TWO: PAYOFF SCENES

Scene: "Training and Seduction"

Purpose: To show their expertise as thieves and that they have feelings for each other.

Analysis: That would be the official purpose, but since we've already seen their expertise previously, there really isn't much point in seeing it again. Therefore, while the grid of red string with bells attached to simulate laser alarms is a cool visual, it's not enough to carry the amount of time the audience spends in an unnecessary scene. So the payoff would have to be the second purpose: the development of their feelings for each other. But that, too, is weak because too much time is spent focusing on watching CZJ in a skintight, Mrs. Peel outfit, slithering sensually around the red string. While that does indeed show that she's sexy (something else the audience already knows), the implication here is that SC is falling for her because she's sexy, not for any other character attributes. This results in both of them being shallow. Again, the writers took the obvious and less interesting approach.

Grade: B-.

Scene: "Phone Call, Betrayal and Castle Top"

Purpose: This is a *continuous scene* in that three short scenes are strung together in rapid succession because they are closely linked. In this case, the purpose is the traditional Act Two *complicating factor*. CZJ leaves SC's remote castle under the pretense of buying SC a gift. As soon as she sees a phone booth, she calls Will Patton to tell him she's got SC hooked into stealing the mask and now they can catch him red-handed. Complication #1: Does the audience believe that she will betray SC? Complication #2: WP is angry at her for not contacting him sooner. The audience can see that he doesn't trust her. What will he do about it? Complication #3: The audience sees SC listening in on the phone conversation; now they know he knows her plan. Does he believe she'll betray him or the insurance company?

Analysis: Solid, if uninspired. It's basically another talking-heads scene made interesting by the levels of betrayal going on and the quaint Scottish village setting. There is an attempt to add a touch of suspense to counter the otherwise static scene: SC lures her to the top of his castle, gets her close to the edge overlooking the craggy shore and choppy sea below and then, with a scowl, talks about how he never comes up here without throwing something over. There's a long, suspenseful pause, then he tosses his brandy glass over. The thinking is that the structure calls for an intense suspense moment here. However, does anyone really think he's going to toss her off halfway through the movie? Given that, it's a useless and silly scene.

Grade: Phone call, B; castle top, C-. Good complication, bad suspense.

Scene: "Stealing the Mask"

Purpose: It's the tent-pole payoff scene. The two expert thieves must work together to steal the priceless mask from an impenetrable building. The audience sees them do just what they've practiced, executed flawlessly.

Analysis: The scene is not executed flawlessly. Too much time is spent watching CZJ doing all those same sensual movements the audience already saw her do in training. The lengthy repetition reduces the suspense at a time when it should be increasing. Also, once again the theft is too easily done with absolutely no threat of them getting caught. There is a lone guard patrolling, but never does the audience fear he'll get there in time. Had he, it would have been an opportunity to show the two thieves improvising, working together, using their different strengths as a team. The reason it is so crucial that their heist has problems is to establish that things can go wrong; they aren't perfect. This will make the main heist of the story in Act Three more suspenseful because the audience knows things can go wrong. Another problem is that immediately during their escape after this heist, SC repeatedly plunges CZJ's head underwater until she tells him whose side she's on. Once again, does the audience believe he'll really drown her? But if he'd arranged it so she was trapped in the building with the guards coming and only he could help her escape before getting caught, there would have been suspense. The audience would believe he might let her get caught, especially after hearing her phone call. In fact, what if he had let her get caught and then visited her in disguise to get the truth, cleverly arranging her escape as a reward? That would have shown the audience how ruthless he could be, which would have increased the stakes for Act Three. And the audience would know that if he's betrayed by her, he's willing to carry through with his threats.

Grade: C+. It has potential, but it never builds the stakes.

ACT THREE: PAYOFF SCENES
Scene: "Near-Sex"
Purpose: To show how much he cares for her so the audience is surprised by the twist in the Dénouement Scene (to come). After discovering SC has stolen the mask from her, CZJ rages at SC, clubbing and screaming at him. Afterward, they embrace. She wants sex, but he refuses for reasons, he says, that are too complicated to explain to her. However, they do cuddle on the floor, with him looking troubled.

Analysis: Although it's hard to believe anyone refusing to have sex with a willing CZJ, the fact that he does indicates that he has a strong reason not to. The implication is that his reason is moral, which accomplishes two things: It makes the audience like him more and anxious to know what that reason could be.

Grade: B. Her explosion of emotion is unexpected and so is his refusal of her. It renews the audience's hope that the story, which so far has made too many familiar choices, still may have some unexpected twists for the ending.

Scene: "Computer Heist"
Purpose: To show the final climactic heist that the whole

movie has been promising. This time they are going to steal eight billion dollars by breaking into a computer and having it deposit the money in a secret account. In an action-thriller like this, much of the audience's appreciation for the film relies on this one scene. It must be exciting, suspenseful and clever.

Analysis: Pretty good. The idea of the heist is a bit complex, but clever (involving stealing ten seconds from the international clock in order to carry out this heist). The stakes are high because Will Patton is on the scene with a vengeance. He's seen photos of SC hugging CZJ, so now he wants to nail both of them. And there are two earlier scenes in which SC's henchman (Ving Rhames) both threatens SC, who wants to abandon this heist, and betrays him to WP. This time things go wrong and there's a lot of chasing around and daring action. The climax of the action scene is the two thieves traversing the cable under a covered walkway that connects two skyscrapers. They're hanging by a cable that suddenly begins to unravel, then the bolts holding the cable pop out. (This is traditionally what happens when protagonists hang on ropes or cables over long plunges to certain death.) So not only is it predictable, but a little unbelievable that these two pros would risk hanging from a cable that wasn't thick enough.

Grade: B.

Scene: "Dénouement and Escape"

Purpose: To explain all of the twists in the plot and allow the "lovers" to escape together.

Analysis: Fair. The audience wants them to escape together, so all the writer has to do is make it plausible. Unfortunately, this is a bit lacking. The scene takes place on a train platform on which there are no other travelers. All the major characters are here. Explanations are given and the audience realizes how clever and complex the plot was. That part is good. But then, just as CZJ is supposed to be arrested, SC whispers to her, slips her a gun and she holds it to his head so the cops will stay away while she hops on the train and escapes. This escape scene is crucial because the way it's done is the last memory of the film's cleverness the audience will have, but it's so simplistic and unbelievable that it disappoints. Finally, she returns, they gaze lovingly into each other's eyes and the trains pass between the audience and the characters; when the trains are gone, so are they. Vanished. Most of the people in the script workshop complained that this was too corny. Not only was it familiar, but it didn't satisfy. The audience needed a longer dialogue scene with some kind of closure with the characters.

Grade: B-.

(*Note*: Notice how each act ends with a major action scene. These are the payoff moments of each act, designed to heighten the audience's participation and provide momentum for compelling them through the next less active scenes.)

Final Word

What we did with *Entrapment* is what every writer should do with his own story, novel or script. First, outline it with note cards, then study them. By looking at the skeleton of the story, you are better able to distance yourself from the work. Just reading the scenes over and over won't be enough. You will get distracted by your own prose style, by all of your revisions, by the ideas in your head that may have never made it to paper. Study the cards and analyze the scenes just as we did above. Obviously, different genres will require different structures: A suspense story needs some action scenes while a mainstream literary novel may not. However, the literary novel does require payoff scenes and the note cards will help determine if there are enough of them, if they come in the best possible locations and if they are as compelling as they might be.

Rarely do scenes or chapters stay in the same order you thought they'd be in. I don't think I've ever written a novel in which I didn't rearrange scenes for greater impact. When Ann Beattie finished her novel, *Love Always*, she laid out the chapters on her living room floor and reassembled them "like pieces in a puzzle."

Sometimes it isn't until your child is grown that you have the distance to look at the whole person and judge what kind of job you did raising her, how much was your responsibility, how much was genetic hardwiring and how much was just dumb luck.

✸ 15 ✸
FROM FIRST TO
FINAL DRAFT:
REVISING

> *"I think to understand an idea you have to wade in, write your way through it, and throw away big hunks until you get it right.... I think of a story not as a part of myself on a page, but as a thing that can be better or worse depending on what I do to it. I really do think of it as a thing to be shaped, made, and perfected."*
>
> Lee Smith
> author of *Me and My Baby View the Eclipse*

> *"First drafts are for learning what your novel or story is about. Revision is working with that knowledge to enlarge and enhance an idea, to re-form it.... Revision is one of the true pleasures of writing."*
>
> Bernard Malamud

I have a little writing secret that has seen me through the completion of over thirty-five books, ten screenplays and dozens of stories and poems. Just when I'm most frustrated with my daily writing and the demons of common sense are whispering, "Find another profession, you no-talented hack," I summon up this little secret and the demons vanish like relatives after you announce you need to borrow money.

My secret is this: My first few drafts are always crap. Guaranteed.

This is not self-deprecation or false modesty. I know when I sit down to write the first few versions of a chapter, story or article, that whatever appears on the screen is a far cry from what I'm imagining in my mind. But that doesn't bother me anymore because I know I can fix it. I have come to learn that good writing has nothing to do with the first, third or fiftieth draft. In fact, good writing has to do with *not* counting drafts, *not* keeping track of how many times you've revised something. The only draft that counts is the final draft.

This is the last chapter of the book because it is the most important. The other chapters teach you how to write various specific scenes, but this chapter is about how to put all of those separate scenes together to form the whole work, which is the point of it all.

Getting to "The End"

Revising can be daunting. There's so much to look for—pacing, characterization, plot, theme, style, etc.—that a writer can get lost in the labyrinthine process. The difference between the early and final drafts of writing is that early drafts lay down the basic story and characters while the final drafts fine-tune what is already there. The early stages of writing and revising resemble first aid on a battlefield: you see a gaping wound (such as a clichéd description) and you slap a Band-Aid on it (change a few words). This is because early drafts are part of the discovery process. This is when the writing is most liquid, when you can feel free to add or delete passages, go in a different direction than you had first intended or suddenly expand minor characters into major ones. You can be more daring because the area is still uncharted. But once you have charted it—that is, once you have the characters you want, doing and saying the things you want, in the order you want—now you're ready for the final drafts. Early drafts are like selecting the members of a sports team; final drafts are teaching them to play together as one cooperative unit.

Although the phrase "final draft" suggests that it's the last time you'll revise, that really isn't the case. Final draft really refers to the final *process* of revising. It's when you are satisfied with the basics but now want to erase any persistent flaws. Sometimes the process is minor—just touch-up painting here and there. Sometimes it's more major—knocking out walls and adding windows.

Ground Rules

The key to successful final revisions is to *compartmentalize your approach*. Instead of trying to revise all of the aspects of the text at once, concentrate only on one element at a time. The following five-step method of revision is a simple way to examine each of the most crucial elements. The strength of this method is that by doing only one step at a time, you are fully focused on that area and not distracted by other problems. Don't give in to the temptation to fix something that is not part of the step you are pursuing. If you're revising for dialogue and come across a choppy narrative passage, just mark the passage and return to it later when you are concentrating on narration. Keep in mind that each step has an ultimate goal and achieving that goal is the whole point of a particular revision.

The other important element to remember is *to apply this process only on short, self-contained sections*. If you're revising a long story or novel, use this method on scenes or chapters. My students always ask if they can't just keep writing ahead rather than revise scenes or chapters as they go along, then fix everything once they've completed the entire first draft. Although I am usually very much against any "rules of writing" because each writer must find the method that works best for him or her, I strongly discourage the method of writing the full draft and then going back to revise. The reason is that the act of revising is not just applying makeup and accessories. Sometimes it involves rethinking what you're writing about, what you want to say, who these characters are and where you're going with the story. Sometimes you only discover the answers to these questions during a rewrite. There's usually a reason you get stuck in a particular place: You realize something is wrong with what you've written or intend to write, but you don't know what that something is. You need to take the time to figure out what element is bothering you in order to know what comes next. Pay attention to this crucial instinct because it's the writer's gag reflex: It keeps you from swallowing bad writing.

Also, by not writing ahead, you'll feel more free to follow

any of the many options you have, whether that involves eliminating major characters, changing settings or drastically altering the plot. Sometimes you may even end up changing protagonists. (After writing ninety pages of *The Thin Man*, Dashiell Hammett dumped his popular Continental Op protagonist and replaced him with Nick and Nora Charles.) But once you've written ahead and have already structured the whole story, you have a greater commitment to keep what you've already written. Now, instead of experimenting with all of the options for improving your story, you're more likely to try to build bridges to force scenes to meet.

Revising calls for a certain degree of ruthlessness. You must question the worthiness of every aspect that's in your story, and if anything is found wanting, you must jettison it. The following steps will help you find those weak spots and offer some suggestions of how to fix or cut them.

STEP 1: STRUCTURE
Goal: Develop a clear and compelling plot.

Problems to Look For: (1) too passive/talking heads and (2) no buildup/anticlimactic.

How to Fix: We start here because structure is the skeleton of the scene. Once these bones are all correctly aligned, stuffing the internal organs in the right place and stretching the skin over it is a lot easier. Basically, you're looking to see that the plot events are in the right order and, if they are, that the scene builds toward a satisfying climactic payoff.

The passive/talking-heads scene occurs when characters are sitting around yammering back and forth without any tension to the scene. They are called talking heads not because they're speaking a lot, but because what they're saying seems removed from any sense of characterization. It's as if they are puppets speaking the words of the author rather than real people speaking their own minds.

One simple way to fix this is to change the setting so that the scene is more active. Instead of the husband and wife sitting in the airport waiting for his mother to arrive while discussing how horrible she is, put them in a car stuck in horrendous airport traffic that may make them late. This additional element is a misdirection device, shifting the reader's focus to the urgency of the couple being late, which makes the reader anxious and more apt to pay attention to the dialogue. Also, it gives the couple more to talk about (the awful traffic, his or her bad driving), so the conversation seems less contrived and more natural. And it gives a concrete focus to the mother's character by introducing the fact that she hates it when people are late; this fact *shows* the reader who she is and takes the place of long descriptions of how controlling she is. The son can even throw in an anecdote about something outrageous the mother did when someone was late (e.g., stood up and left the hospital because the surgeon was late; or left her daughter's wedding because the groom was late).

Each scene is like a ministory: It has a beginning, middle and ending. The beginning introduces the conflict of the scene, the middle complicates it and the ending resolves it. That means every scene has to have a "hot spot," a point in which the action and/or emotions reach an apex. Usually the scene builds towards this. When revising for structure, make sure you locate the hot spot and make sure it generates enough heat to justify the scene's existence. You'll know if it has enough heat if the reader's anticipation is satisfied during this moment. One of the main reasons scenes weaken here is that writers end the scene too early, as if it were a TV series and they were breaking for commercial. An argument doesn't end when someone makes a witty or stinging comment—it keeps on going to the point where people are uncomfortable, frustrated, at a loss for words. So must the scene.

So far I've discussed revising structure within a scene or chapter. However, once the whole story is completed, you must also revise the structure of the larger work: Make sure all of the scenes are in the best order. It can also mean eliminating some scenes. You have to do what's best for the whole work, even if it means cutting a wonderful scene that no longer fits. John Steinbeck once warned writers to "Beware of a scene that becomes too dear to you, dearer than the rest."

Before moving scenes around, I suggest you create note cards for each scene or chapter (see chapter fourteen for details). Tack them up in order on your bulletin board. Now you

have a clearer visual sense of the rhythm of the story. Do you
have too many passive scenes together, thereby dampening the
momentum? Are the settings too similar? Just by studying the
cards, you can sometimes discover structure problems. Move
the cards around and see if changing the order of the scene
helps. Or perhaps you'll notice that you need an additional
scene between a couple of characters. If so, the note cards will
help show you where to add the scene.

STEP 2: TEXTURE

Goal: Sharpen descriptive passages to make the characters,
setting and action more vivid.

What to Look For: (1) too much or too little description, (2)
clichéd word choices, (3) too many adjectives, (4) a research information dump and (5) information in the wrong place.

How to Fix: This step has a lot to do with defining your
own unique style. Some writers use a lot of description, others
use very little. There's no right way. But when there's so much
description that the story's momentum bogs down, that's too
much. Or if there's so little that the characters or settings are
bland and unmemorable, that's too little. Most writers, myself
included, have many descriptive passages that they love, but
wisely cut from a story because the passages call too much attention to themselves and detract from the story. Any time you
see a passage of description that is so poetic and involving that
the reader stops to admire the author, cut it. You've just intruded into the story to take a bow, thereby smothering your
own creation. Save all of those wonderful passages you cut in
a folder; you may be able to use them in other stories.

On the other hand, telling the reader too little can be
equally annoying. While some writers insist on telling us every
detail of a character's description and background, right down
to the number of freckles on her ear and where she bought her
blouse (Bloomingdale's during a Memorial Day sale, reduced
from $98 to $38 because of a slight stain on the sleeve), others
are stingy with any details. The reader emerges from a scene
not having any idea of the characters' ages or physical description, or a feel for the settings. Even though the writer may tell
the reader that the scene takes place in an alley, he never expe-

riences the alley and is never fully involved in the scene. The danger in fixing this problem is to overdescribe by assaulting the reader's senses with every sight, smell, sound, taste and feel of the alley. Instead, concentrate on one aspect: "The alley bordered several low-cost restaurants competing for the lunch money of the secretaries on a budget in nearby office buildings. The cloying smell of things being fried—french fries, tempura, extra-crispy chicken—lay trapped between the buildings like a heavy fog. Randy was grateful for that aggressive odor, otherwise he'd have to deal with whatever was spilling out of all those Dumpsters, especially the one with the chicken feet sticking out like branches from under the lid." In this case, focusing on the smell provides enough texture, while also implying visuals: the types of food being fried tell the reader what kind of restaurants they are. Ending with a visual snapshot of the chicken legs provides the emotional reaction that the writer wants, something that couldn't be achieved if the reader was flooded with too many visual details.

Directly related to this is the dreaded "information dump" described in chapter three. This is where the writer decides to stop the story cold in order to give a lot of details about the history of the house the characters live in or how to pilot a plane. Yes, sometimes those details are not only important to your story, but they add a level of credibility. Novice writers tend to include either too much information or too many such passages. Scenes that involve technical information should remain short.

Aside from adjusting length, writers can vastly improve the impact of the texture by concentrating on word choices. Read entirely through the manuscript one time during which the only thing you do is circle words that could be stronger. Then go back and take your time replacing them. Do not rely on a thesaurus; many times you'll just be replacing one dull word for a more complex and even duller word. The word you're looking for often isn't a synonym, it's just something richer and more evocative.

A common reason that passages can bog down or lose their snap is that the writer has burdened it with too many adjectives. The beginner's logic is that if one adjective is good, three is great. Not so. Clustering adjectives together actually causes them to do battle with each other, one devouring the other until none has any impact. Most of the time when there are several adjectives together, at least two of them have the same meaning anyway. For example: "She was a quiet, introspective, shy girl." Do we need all those adjectives, especially since they are quite similar in meaning? Think of every adjective as a hundred-dollar bill and spend wisely. Read through the manuscript one time doing nothing but cutting unnecessary adjectives. Neither add or replace anything this time through, only cut.

STEP 3: DIALOGUE

Goal: Elicit character personality through conversation.

What to Look For: (1) too many tag lines, (2) too few tag lines, (3) tag lines in the wrong place, (4) tag lines that contain too much information, (5) yet another information dump and (6) bland or melodramatic lines.

How to Fix: The first four areas to examine involve the use of tag lines, which are the "he said" and "she said" parts of dialogue. Basically, the tag line identifies the speaker, such a simple task that you wouldn't think it could be such a big deal. Yet the misuse of tag lines is one of the most destructive forces in dialogue. Some beginning writers feel that every line of dialogue requires a tag line. It doesn't. If there are only two speakers, several lines of pure dialogue can go on without ever telling the reader who the speaker is; he already knows. The proliferation of tag lines is really nothing more than lazy writing, used as a crutch to avoid making the characters' voices so individual that the reader can recognize their cadence and tone without being told. This is because beginning writers focus too much on *what* the characters are saying and not enough on *how* they are saying it.

There are times, however, when the reader does have to be told who is speaking. This may be necessary because there are several speakers, or the dialogue is interspersed with action or interior monologues, or just for the sake of the rhythm of the writing. Following are several examples of the same line of dialogue, each presented with a variation on the same tag line.

Notice the subtle differences in the effect achieved by each.

> *"Hi," she said, moving toward me.*
> *"Hi," she said. She moved toward me.*
> *She moved toward me. "Hi."*
> *"Hi." She moved toward me.*

The first two examples are friendlier because the "she said" slows the pace, taking away some of the energy from her act of moving. The second two examples are more dramatic because they present just the dialogue and the action, which now seems more deliberate and aggressive. (*A note about word choice*: What does the word "move" imply here that "walk" doesn't? "Move" is less visual than "walk," but more sensual, implying that she is more of a force than just an average person, someone whom the narrator has some nervousness about as she approaches.)

Where the tag line goes affects the emphasis on the dialogue. Look at the following variations. Which has more impact?

> *"This is yours. That is not," he said.*
> *"This is yours," he said. "That is not."*

The second version is stronger because the emphasis is now on "That is not." Placing the emphasis there adds an ominous tone. The first version has the lines together, which doesn't emphasize either statement and makes the dialogue seem breezier.

Another common error is placing the tag line at the end of a long speech. For example:

> *"I just don't know what to do about James. He's always running around with delinquent types, like those nasty boys from over in Springfield, the ones with gun racks in their trucks and beer cans under their car seats," Tina said.*

There are two problems with this: (1) If the reader doesn't know who the speaker is until he gets to the end of the speech, then he's going to be confused while reading it; if he does know, then no tag line is necessary. (2) Even while reading the speech, the reader can see there's a tag line, so he doesn't fully commit to the dialogue until he sees how the tag line will affect how he should view the speech. This problem can easily be solved by relocating the tag line:

> *"I just don't know what to do about James," Tina said. "He's always running around with delinquent types, like those nasty boys from over in Springfield, the ones with gun racks in their trucks and beer cans under their car seats."*

Now the reader knows who the speaker is up front and when he finishes reading the speech, he is left with a vivid image of the nasty boys with gun racks and beer cans, not of Tina speaking. If you are going to use a tag line in a long speech, do so as soon as stylistically possible. If you wait too long, the reader won't know who the speaker is until the end and you will have broken the rhythm.

Sometimes you need to identify the speaker, but you don't want to use the word "said" for the millionth time. You can substitute an action instead. This still identifies the speaker but adds a visual image. The first two of the following examples are the usual "said" variations; the third demonstrates substituting an action.

> *"You always do this to me," I said.*
> *I said, "You always do this to me."*
> *I shook my head. "You always do this to me."*

Don't overdo this technique, otherwise every line of dialogue will have a gesture attached to it and the characters will all seem like they're on a caffeine buzz.

Finally, keep your tags simple. The more complex the tag line, the more it detracts from the actual dialogue. Avoid adverbs, e.g. "She said angrily." Every time you see a word with an "ly" at the end, scrutinize it to make sure it's necessary. In general, adverbs are often repetitious; the dialogue tells us she's angry, so there's no need to repeat it.

Information dumps appear with alarming frequency in the dialogue of weak writers. It's pretty much the same problem as described above under "Texture." Here characters ramble on about the history of their family or how to make cheese. This same information can be compelling as long as it doesn't seem as if the author intruded just to unload all of his research. Instead of having a lengthy monologue with one character spewing forth, let the information come out as part of the conversation. Perhaps the speaker is reluctant to tell the information but the listener wheedles it out of him. Or the speaker is blabby and the listener keeps trying to shut him up. Or the conversation takes place while the characters are doing something else that allows for interruptions: maybe they're at a garage sale looking for vintage bowling shirts or on a ski lift preparing to ski down the steepest mountain they've ever been on. Now you have parallel topics, with one being the misdirection, the other being the real information you want to get across.

Punching up bland or melodramatic dialogue is tricky because you have to be able to recognize it. You may think that if someone knew what bad dialogue was, they wouldn't write it in the first place. It's not that simple. A line of dialogue doesn't exist in a vacuum; its power comes from the context, from the lines around it, the situation that prompts it, the character who says it. A line in one context may seem bland, but in another context it may be brilliant. Some minor tinkering can sharpen a line. Here's an example from a student manuscript:

> *"I'll see if I can do a trade so we can sit together."*
> *"I'd like that," Susan said, "but I'd be rotten company."*
> *"We can be rotten together," he said.*

Not a bad line. It's meant to endear him to her. But a better line would be: "We can rot together." It's less expected and therefore a bit funnier, edgier, suggesting a character who isn't as predictable.

One of the things I do before editing my own dialogue is read a passage by someone whose dialogue I admire, for example, Elmore Leonard, Ross Thomas, Lorrie Moore, Jane Smiley and Peter de Vries. Don't limit yourself to just fiction writers. Reading playwrights like Beth Henley and David Mamet is also extremely helpful. Which writer I choose to read depends on the tone that I want to achieve. If the scene calls for fast-paced, edgy dialogue, I may read Leonard. If I want playful and desperate, I may read Mamet. Whomever you choose, don't read an entire story or play. Just read the dialogue passages until you have a feel for the language, then immediately go to work and start editing. In addition, John Steinbeck advised writers to say the dialogue aloud as they write it: "Only then will it have the sound of speech."

Step 4: Editing
Goal: Tighten pace and continuity.
What to Look For: (1) repetition through implication and (2) slow passages.
How to Fix: Cut. Cut. Cut. This is often the hardest part for writers because they've worked so hard on every word, but this step is the one that gives the work its final shape. Much of what you will cut is repetition, words that repeat what the reader already knows because it's been said directly or implied elsewhere. Nobel Prize-winning writer I.B. Singer once said, "The writer's best friend is the wastepaper can." Apply this maxim to individual words and lines, and you have the essence of editing. The following passage is an early draft from a student novel—literary mainstream. Susan and Bill are coincidentally on the same flight back to their hometown. They have feelings for each other, though not yet spoken. Draw a line through all of the words you'd cut.

"Uncle Jake's had a heart attack."
"No!" ~~Shock and regret clouded his face.~~
"Harry Tobin called me." The muffled drone of airplane engines, the smell of jet fuel and the odors of fast food and lavatory deodorizers ~~were a sudden assault on her senses. She felt~~ queasy. "I've been shuttling all over the eastern half of this country since ten o'clock last night, trying to get the quickest connection home."
"I'm so sorry about Jake," Bill said. "How serious is it?"
They fell into stride, hurrying toward the gate.

> ~~"I'm not really sure," she said.~~ "Harry said it was bad.
> When I called the hospital from Memphis, I couldn't get any
> information except 'guarded.'" She looked over at him, ~~a wan
> smile barely turning up the corners of her mouth. Then it was
> her turn to look more closely.~~ "You look grim. I take it things
> didn't go well?"
>
> "Worse than not well." He kept his face forward. "But no
> comparison with your news."
>
> "What happened?" ~~Immediately she apologized.~~ "Sorry. I
> think this is where you tell me MYOB."

Let's look at the same passage after editing. The words with
strikethroughs have been cut; the underlined words have been
added.

> "Uncle Jake's had a heart attack."
>
> "No!" Shock and regret clouded his face.
>
> "Harry Tobin called me." The muffled drone of airplane
> engines, the smell of jet fuel and the odors of fast food and lava-
> tory deodorizers were a sudden assault on her senses. She felt
> made her queasy. "I've been shuttling all over the eastern half
> of this country since ten o'clock last night, trying to get the
> quickest connection home."
>
> "I'm so sorry about Jake," Bill said. "How serious is it?"
>
> They fell into stride, hurrying toward the gate.
>
> "I'm not really sure," she said. "Harry said it was bad.
> When I called the hospital from Memphis, I couldn't get any
> information except 'guarded.'" She looked over at him, a wan
> smile barely turning up the corners of her mouth. Then it was
> her turn to look more closely. "You look grim. I take it things
> didn't go well?"
>
> "Worse than not well." He kept his face forward. "But no
> comparison with your news."
>
> "What happened?" Immediately she apologized. She
> shook her head at her nosiness. "Sorry. I think this is where
> you tell me MYOB."

Here's why these cuts were made: (1) His exclamation of "No!"
tells the reader he's shocked, and regret is implied because the

reader knows from previous scenes that he likes Jake; (2) the fact that she gets queasy implies the assault on her senses; (3) "Harry said it was bad" is a strong line—the cut line weakens the speech; (4) the "wan smile" description is distracting because it focuses the reader's attention on her face rather than the emotions of the moment; and (5) the reader knows she apologizes because he sees the word "sorry." No need to tell the reader. However, the writer's instincts are correct in that there needs to be a rhythmic break there. Instead, she could insert an action that is related to her feeling. This makes it more vivid.

Once you have finished editing your manuscript, go through again to make sure there are clear transitions bridging where you have cut. Think you've cut enough? Kaye Gibbons (*Ellen Foster*), after writing her new novel for eighteen months, deliberately deleted all nine hundred pages, explaining, "It was so bad, and it kept being bad."

Step 5: Blending
Goal: Search and destroy any weaknesses.
Problems to Look For: Soft spots: unclear character motivations, actions that seem contrived, etc.
How to Fix: A month ago, a student of mine came to the house with her novel manuscript in hand, desperate because she seemed unable to fix some of the problems that were bothering her. I'd read the novel before, so I was familiar with the story. As she poured out all of the problems in a rush of frustration and anxiety, I stopped her after the first problem and told her how to fix it: Add a scene early in the novel that showed a certain characteristic of the character. She wanted a stronger motivation for why the boy keeps a secret. All she had to do was make the secret bigger than the one she'd created. When she went to the next problem, the solution was the same: Either add a new scene or expand an old one that made the reader believe the thing that happened later. Then I told her to make a written list of what she thought all the problems were and see how many could be addressed merely by changing.

The other day I read a former student's screenplay. He was concerned about whether or not there was enough suspense regarding the main character's quest. I suggested adding a scene in which the character tries to use his new abilities, but fails. This heightens the suspense about the next time he tries.

I recently faced the same situation. An editor said he liked my novel but didn't believe the character was capable of the violence he eventually commits. I suggested adding an early scene that is either a flashback or memory of a youthful indiscretion in which he was violent and how he overcame those tendencies. Fortunately, that addition worked to our advantage in a couple of additional ways.

This blending process is a sort of spot-welding. You find the troubled areas and add new scenes or expand old ones to fix anything you missed. Don't be embarrassed that you missed these things. All writers have to go back and do this same kind of repair work in order for the final product to blend together seamlessly.

Final Word

There is no such creature as the final draft. It is as mythological as the unicorn. Just when you think you're done with a manuscript, you take another look at it and suddenly you're scribbling notes on every page. However, there is a point at which every manuscript must be abandoned, sent out to publishers and the next work begun. This five-step revision method will allow you to reach that "final" draft more comfortably because you know you will have examined every aspect possible. But if you've completed these five steps and still feel the work needs something, begin again with step one. You can apply these five steps more than once to the same manuscript. I do.

Eventually, you must kick it out of the nest to see if it will fly. This is the final—and most difficult—step a writer takes, but it must be taken. Once you've sent the manuscript out to the agent, magazine editor or book publisher of your choice, don't sit around waiting to see what will happen. Begin your next work as soon as possible. Not only will it distract you from the waiting, but all of the techniques you've just learned and practiced in the completed manuscript are fresh in your mind and will make this next work even better.

It is the lot of writers to constantly question whether or not they have any talent. A book like this, with so much advice, may seem overwhelming: "So much to learn, can I ever take it all in? Maybe I'm just not talented." Don't let yourself off the hook that easily. I often tell my students that talent is a resource of limited value. Through the years, I have seen many richly talented writers give up because they lacked the will to finish what was only promising. At the same time, I have seen many moderately talented writers complete novels and screenplays and sell them, and then go on to write others, all of the time becoming better and better writers. James Baldwin thought will was the crucial element to a writer: "Do this book, or die. You have to go through that. Talent is insignificant. I know a lot of talented ruins. Beyond talent lie all the usual words: discipline, love, luck, but, most of all, endurance."

TIP

A Little Editing Help From Your Friends

During the course of completing a story, you should show it to as many qualified people as possible. Qualified means: (1) people who read a lot, especially within the genre you're writing in; (2) people attending workshops; (3) teachers; (4) agents; and (5) editors. Agents and editors should see it last, after you've shown it around, received feedback and made any changes you think are appropriate. Showing it to other people means they will give you their opinions—that's the point. Yet many writers go ballistic when they get their story back and the person offers suggestions. What they really wanted was someone to say, "It's perfect. The most moving, funny, life-changing work I've ever read." I can tell you right now, unless it's your immediate family commenting, that won't happen. Instead of resisting editing advice, examine it as objectively as possible. If it makes sense, use it. If it doesn't, ignore it. But be open to it. I show all of my work to my wife, who is one of the best writers and editors I've ever known. Still, when she is finished reading and is reciting her list of suggested changes, I'm nodding on the outside while inside my mind is shouting, "What's wrong with you! Can't you recognize my genius? What kind of idiotic suggestions are these? Let's see you write the damn book!" And so on. However, I then take the list, read it over, think about it and change whatever I agree with, which is usually somewhere between 50 to 80 percent of what she said. Every book I've written that she's critiqued has been significantly improved because of her suggestions.

❧ INDEX ❧